KIKUYU

DISTRICT

KIKUYU DISTRICT

Francis Hall's letters from East Africa to his father, Lt. Colonel Edward Hall, 1892-1901

Edited & Introduced
by
Paul Sullivan

Mkuki na Nyota Publishers
PO Box 4246
Dar es Salaam, Tanzania
www.mkukinanyota.com

This book is published by :
Mkuki na Nyota Publishers Ltd
P. O. Box 4246
Dar es Salaam, Tanzania
Email: sales.mauzo@mkukinanyota.com
         editorial.uhariri@mkukinanyota.com
Website: www.mkukinanyota.com

Copyright © Paul Sullivan, 2006

ISBN 9987-417-57-4

All rights reserved. No part of this publication may be reproduced, stored in a retrieval system, or transmitted, in any form or by any means, without the prior permission of the publisher, or be otherwise circulated in any form of binding or cover other than that in which it is published and without a similar condition being imposed on the subsequent purchaser.

Contents

List of maps and photographs iv

Acknowledgements v

Introduction viii

1. By ship to Mombasa, on foot to Fort Smith 1
2. Making friends in Kikuyuland 19
3. Encounters with missionaries & rhinos 45
4. Attacked by a leopard 73
5. Convalescence in England 99
6. Back in harness 105
7. Queen Victoria's Jubilee 117
8. Home leave 137
9. Gathering mushrooms by moonlight 139
10. Nairobi, a tin-pot mushroom township 159

Afterword 177

List of Maps and Photographs

Maps

1. East Africa Protectorates, Provinces & Districts 1892 ix
2. British East Africa on completion of the railway xvii
3. Kenya Coast & hinterland 18
4. Kikuyu District 43
5. Distribution of major tribes. British East Africa, 1892 71

Photographs

1. Fort Smith, Kikuyu 87
2. Group at Fort Smith 88
3. Xmas at Kikuyu 89
4. Group at Fort Smith 90
5. Group at Fort Smith 91
6. Caravan at Fort Smith 92
7. Chief Kinyanjui 93
8. Steam engine and railway crew 94
9. Man-eating lion 95
10. Nairobi panorama 96
11. Kikuyu Station 97
12. Fort Machakos 98
13. Francis Hall's grave 98

Acknowledgements

I came across the microfilm reels of Francis Hall's letters in the Kenya National Archives while researching the early days of colonial settlement in East Africa. It proved impossible to download or print the letters and the only option was to transcribe them by hand.

Mr Richard Ambani of the Kenya National Archives suggested that his cousin Mary Atsing'a Okwomi might agree to copy the letters. It took three months of labour and she filled fifteen A4 tablets of paper at five Shillings a page. Without this heroic effort Kikuyu District would not exist.

Jan Hemsing is an authority on East Africa who offered priceless information and constant support. She was never in doubt about the importance of the letters and we enjoyed a memorable safari to find and photograph Francis Hall's grave in the middle of Muranga town.

Patrick Kirby is another long term enthusiastic supporter of Francis Hall's book and has drawn the maps and designed the cover with his customary flair and skill. I thank them both for keeping the flag flying over the years.

The Consolata Fathers were early Catholic missionaries in Kikuyuland and their library in Nairobi is full of treasures. Father Quatrocchio found the early map which is reproduced on the cover and I thank him for his friendly interest in the project and for his prayers.

Thanks also to the staff of the Bodleian Library in Oxford and particularly to those at Rhodes House who showed me Francis Hall's archive and efficiently supplied copies of photographs and the pastel portrait on the cover.

In London the librarian and staff of the Royal Geographical Society allowed me to study maps of the period and were generally most helpful.

Professor Richard Greenfield of the Department of History of the University of Asmara has provided access to books and other source material on Kenya.

In Nairobi I thank James Kamande of the Kenya National Archives, John Sinei, curator of the Kenya Railways museum, the British Institute of East Africa, and Matthew and Lily Wilson who contributed to the design of the book.

In Dar es Salaam Deogratias Simba introduced me to Walter Bgoya who made the admirable decision to publish the book. Thanks are due to Fraternus Lyimo and Mutahi Munyi who both contributed to the design and layout of the book.

In Holland I must thank Martin and Janet Sullivan for vital logistical support at a crucial time.

In the text the original letters have been altered as little as possible. Francis Hall's opinion of the events he observes is sometimes robustly expressed but it should be remembered that he was a Victorian man of the British Empire who wrote letters to his immediate family, not for a wider audience.

Paul Sullivan
Nairobi
July 2006
sullivanpaul@excite.com

Map 1   East Africa Protectorates, Provinces and Districts, 1892.

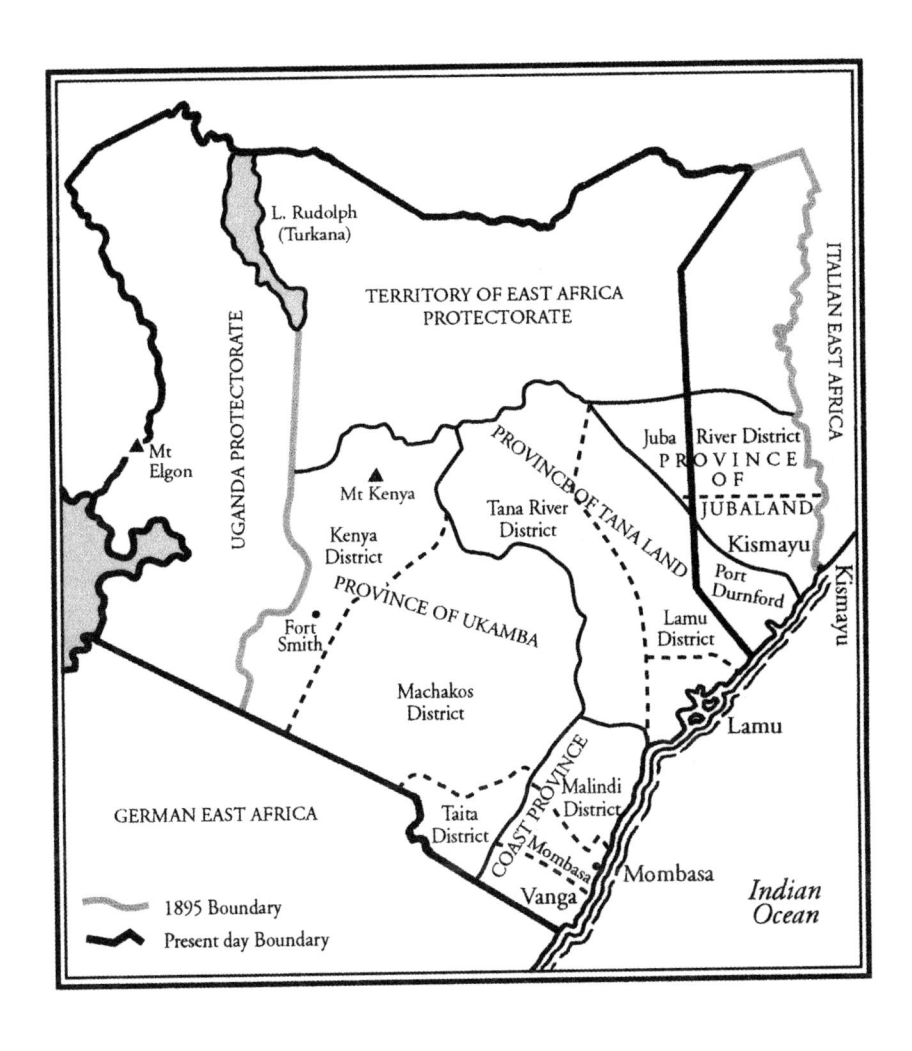

INTRODUCTION

Geologists estimate that three million years ago the height of the volcano now known as Mount Kenya was 23,000 feet. Since then the crater and outer mantle have been eaten away by erosion, leaving only the hard plug of syenite which formed in the centre of the crater as it cooled. Imperceptibly to the eye of man, the mountain has steadily worn away by well over a mile to its present height of 17,058 feet. During the elapsed time between the first European to settle in the country and Kenya's Independence in 1963, and assuming a constant rate of erosion, Mount Kenya's height has been reduced by less than three inches. It is an image that illustrates for just how short a period of time the interior of Africa has been known to Europeans. As recently as 1880 almost nothing was known of the hinterland of East Africa except that it was a source of ivory and slaves.

The first European to make a permanent home in East Africa was the Reverend Dr Johann Ludwig Krapf who established a mission at Rabai Mpia on a hill overlooking Mombasa island in 1844. Two years later he was joined by a fellow German, Johannes Rebmann, to help spread the word of God. Rebmann was the first European to see Kilimanjaro and his report of a snow-capped mountain near the Equator was received with ridicule by the scientific community in England.

The English geographer, W. Desborough Cooley, a pillar of the Royal Geographical Society and acknowledged expert on Africa, scorned Rebmann's claim and dismissed the report as a fraud or a hoax. But Dr Krapf soon confirmed the presence of snow on Kilimanjaro and also reported a second snow-topped peak two hundred miles due north and almost straddling the Equator.

The Wakamba who first pointed out the second mountain to Dr Krapf called it Ki-Nyaa or Kiima Nyaa, the mountain of ostriches, probably because the pattern of black rock and snow on its steep peaks reminded them of the feathers of the cock ostrich. Their name for the mountain was the name later given to the country by British administrators.

In 1882 the Scottish geologist and naturalist Joseph Thomson was invited by the Royal Geographical Society to lead an expedition to find a route from any East African port to Lake Victoria through Maasailand. His mission was to make a map, examine Mount Kenya and make practical observations of the meteorology, geology, natural history and ethnology of the region. Thomson's greatest challenge was passing safely through Maasailand, where the aggressive, marauding tribe of semi-nomadic pastoralists was so feared that their territory was avoided by Arab slavers and Swahili traders alike. Thomson's expedition, his second in East Africa, was a scientific success and an object lesson in man management. Only two porters out of 113 deserted, at a time when the going rate was at least ten percent, and not one shot was fired in anger throughout. He managed the Maasai with a mixture of presents, patience, magic tricks, humour and an ever ready willingness to turn the other cheek. It is doubtful whether more famous explorers such as Stanley, Burton, Speke or Baker would have had the self restraint to cross Maasailand without bloodshed and even Thomson's boyhood hero, the tolerant David Livingstone, may have found the violent Maasai too much of a handful.

The journals of discovery written by such great nineteenth century explorers did much to stimulate European interest in the African continent. Industrialists and traders saw the potential for commercial development in Central Africa; scientists were keen to discover new species and immortalise their name; missionaries and philanthropists were inspired by the prospect of wiping out slavery and the vision of bringing Christianity to millions of Africans.

In the scramble for Africa, the Berlin Conference of 1844-5 sought to regulate the partition of Africa to avoid serious confrontation between the major powers. In the absence of any evidence of occupation in the claimed regions, spheres of influence were recognised.

The British sphere of influence was centred on the spice island of Zanzibar. In 1872 the British India Steam Navigation Company, under the chairmanship of Sir William Mackinnon, established a regular service of mail steamers between Zanzibar and the ports of India and Europe. Sultan Barghash offered Mackinnon a seventy year concession for the administration of Zanzibar and its mainland dominions, including the right of sovereignty, but the Foreign Office dragged its feet and allowed the offer to lapse. Instead, Mackinnon and his partners formed the British East Africa Association, negotiated a fifty year concession with the Sultan, secured sovereign rights for a distance of two hundred miles from the coast, and also concluded twenty one treaties with tribes in the interior.

In April 1888 the Association became the Imperial British East Africa Company (IBEA) and Mackinnon drafted an ambitious list of goals. He planned to administer the entire territory conceded by the Sultan and to acquire more territory from local chiefs by treaty, by purchase or by other means. With an anticipated Charter of Incorporation from the Crown, the IBEA expected to trade, to levy taxes, to grant licences, to coin money, construct roads and public works, and generally to exercise all the rights of sovereignty over the acquired districts.

Mackinnon's enthusiasm for the IBEA was not matched in London, and since Britain herself evaded the responsibility for the land she had claimed as her own, the Company took on the burden of functioning as Britain's surrogate government in East Africa.

Mackinnon championed the idea of a railway from Mombasa to Lake Victoria and the project became one of the Company's main objectives despite inadequate capital. There was much support for the line both inside and outside the British government. The powerful anti-slavery lobby carried the strongest emotional appeal, for it was generally believed that the slave trade could not exist in the presence of a railway line. Despite this argument, slavery remained legal in East Africa until 1907, a fact which F. D. Lugard, an employee of the Company in Uganda called "a gross scandal" and he accused the IBEA and some missionary groups of employing slaves as porters for their safaris. Lugard also noted that a fugitive slave in a British possession had fewer legal rights than an escaped Indian elephant.

The promise of profits was a major incentive for supporters of the railway. East and Central Africa were rich sources of raw materials and it was believed potential for trade definitely existed. For example, ivory was carried by porters from Uganda to the coast for £300 a ton compared with the estimated railway freight charges of £3 a ton.

As unlikely as it sounds, a third factor in favour of the Uganda railway, after anti-slavery and trading, was the security of India. The opening of the Suez canal in 1869 shortened the sailing distance between England and India by seven thousand miles and reduced the passage by forty days. The sudden realisation that the integrity of the canal depended on the headwaters of the Nile caused the Kingdom of Uganda to become incalculably important strategically. Whoever controlled Uganda controlled the Nile; the controller of the Nile ruled Egypt; the ruler of Egypt possessed the Suez canal and held the key to India.

In February 1891 the British Treasury informed Mackinnon that it would guarantee the interest on a paid up capital of £1.25 million, the estimated cost of building a metre gauge railway from Mombasa to Lake Victoria. The IBEA Directors consulted three railway engineers who agreed that the estimate was too low by at least half a million pounds and that a survey was essential to arrive at a reliable figure. To finance the survey of the line, the nearly bankrupt Company cut their costs by recalling Lugard from Uganda and limiting the Company's effective occupation of the territory only as far as Kikuyuland, some 350 miles inland. In November 1891 a 389 man survey expedition led by Captain J R L Macdonald landed in Mombasa and prepared to depart for the interior.

Six months later, in May 1892, thirty two year old Francis George Hall sailed from England in the s.s. Ethiopia bound for Mombasa in the service of the Company. He was the third son of Lieutenant Colonel Edward Hall, late of the 52nd Bengal Native Infantry, and a nephew of Lord Goschen, Chancellor of the Exchequer in Lord Salisbury's Conservative government. Francis Hall was born in Saugor, India on 11th October 1860 and educated at Sherborne and later at Tonbridge. Unsuited by temperament and inclination for office work, he resigned from his first job at the Bank of England and sailed for South Africa in 1880 at the age of twenty with a few pounds in his pocket and sundry letters of introduction to family friends.

At Port Elizabeth he quit his job after two days as a junior clerk for a shipping company, disgusted by the conditions and terms of service. He moved on to King Williams Town where the post of Assistant Master at Dale College suited him better. He was popular with the boys for his prowess in rugby and running but the job was interrupted by the outbreak of the Kaffir rising and Hall joined the King Williams Town Volunteer Mounted Artillery as a 2nd Lieutenant in the Herschel Native Contingent, though he saw no action. At the end of hostilities he secured the position of Assistant Master at Dordrecht public school until January 1883 when he finally ended his career as a teacher.

Then followed a series of failed ventures and desperate attempts to make a living. For a time he was an unsuccessful farmer. He then set up and ran a country store in an out-of-the-way district with a partner who cheated him. In 1885 he served for a year with the Bechuanaland Field Force under Lord Methuen and was awarded a campaign medal with 'Basutoland' clasp for his services. He gave up farming in 1886 and moved to the Rand goldfields where he eked out an existence for eighteen months doing odd jobs - at one time driving a horse drawn cab for a living. The next two and a half years were spent prospecting in the low country by the Murchison range, sinking wells and shafts, accepting any job that came along, including a spell as clerk to a travelling attorney.

After eleven years of hardship and unrewarding struggle hampered by repeated attacks of fever, Hall returned to England from South Africa in 1891. He found it impossible to resist the tug of Africa and leapt at the chance to join the IBEA Company in East Africa, determined to succeed in this new career through sheer hard work and dedication.

Francis Hall's letters to his father are the earliest European record of daily life in British East Africa, the territory that was to become known as Kenya. He was the first European to record camping "on the Nairobi river on the edge of the Kapiti Plains, ten miles from Fort Smith" in June 1893. And although he was an appointed official, Francis Hall was in fact Kenya's first British settler. His personality, temperament, attitude and behaviour made him a settler first and an official second. And unlike Joseph Thomson, Francis Hall came to live in the country, not to explore it, though he explored it thoroughly for the next nine years.

His earlier experience in South Africa was crucial to his success in East Africa. No stranger to the company of Africans, he was an effective man manager and learned Kiswahili quickly as the key to effective communication. Self sufficient, good with his hands and a man of many practical skills, he was obliged to wear several different hats on a daily basis. In addition to his official duties he was a farmer, veterinarian, doctor, nurse, mechanic, surveyor, navigator, road builder, hunter, horseman, carpenter, diplomat, linguist, secretary, scientist, banker, cartographer, meteorologist, policeman, judge, jury, accountant, soldier, supervisor and hotel manager.

In his letters Hall reflects the insecurity of his career as his prospects for promotion and his personal finances fluctuate from month to month. He frequently felt forgotten by the 'powers that be' and envied his brother officers who lived in relative luxury in Mombasa with a Governor-General's ear within easy reach. The frustrations of living in a slow motion bureaucracy must have been immense. It was a nineteen day march to the coast if all went well. A letter from Mombasa took ten days by a relay of mail runners. It took a minimum of three weeks to get an answer to a question or take delivery of anything from a needle to a plough. By the time newspapers arrived from England they were at least seven weeks out of date and it is easy to picture Hall sitting in a long chair reading them in strict chronological order.

An unspoken rivalry developed between Francis Hall and John Ainsworth, his opposite number in Machakos. Appointed four years earlier than Hall, Ainsworth was the quintessential official who delighted in paper work, accounting, memoranda, rules and regulations, all the things that Hall detested. When the railway arrived and Nairobi was created by surveyors and engineers, Fort Smith became redundant almost overnight. Ainsworth saw his chance and claimed Nairobi while Hall was sent to Machakos in Ainsworth's place. Ainsworth outlived Hall, was preferred to him and was decorated for his services. Yet it was the charismatic Francis Hall who had the common touch. It was Hall who kept the peace between the Kikuyu and the Maasai, playing them off against each other skilfully, and securing their personal loyalty and affection separately.

In British East Africa, Francis Hall at last found his place in life. All his varied and diverse experience made him ideally qualified for his job with the IBEA. He was a one man band in the middle of nowhere and sometimes went weeks without speaking English or seeing another European. His letters were therefore an essential means of communication, an outlet for his frustrations and a vehicle for his complaints. And yet despite all his problems, one can sense from his letters, as his father in Tunbridge Wells must have sensed, that Francis Hall loved what he was doing, loved the place where he lived and loved the people he met.

Map 2   British East Africa on completion of the Uganda Railway showing the Coast (1) and Kikuyu District (2)

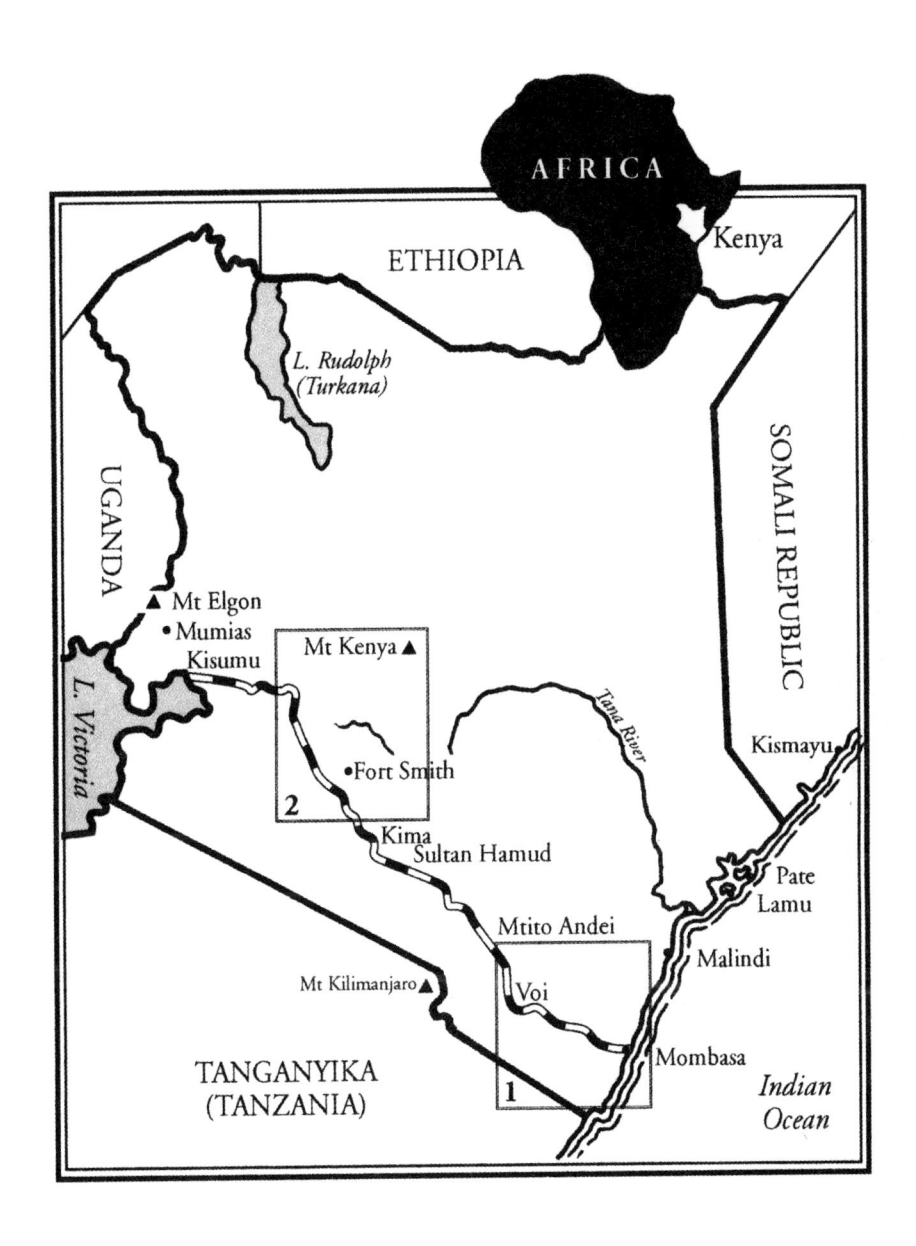

This book is for my mother and in memory of my father.

Chapter One

BY SHIP TO MOMBASA, ON FOOT TO FORT SMITH

Somewhere Mediterranean
Sunday
[s.s. Ethiopia. May 15th 1892]

My Dear Papa,
So far we have had about as uneventful & quiet a voyage as one could think. The sea has been like a mill-pond & I am half afraid that we may miss our letters in Naples as we shall be there before our time & the skipper tells me we shall probably reach Mombasa at least three days before the advertised date.

As Jack[1] will have told you we have a crowd of Missionary people on board belonging to the C.M.S.[2] The society must be pretty flourishing for there are eight of them going out, all first class, & each one has £7 cash given him to spend at ports of call & expenses on the voyage besides £100 each for outfit. This is how they try to civilize the natives.

But I must try to describe the passengers and officers. The skipper is a very jolly fellow, rough & ready, and as he hates Missionaries has chummed up with Schiff & myself & we have a good time. The Chief, second and third mates are all young and very nice fellows & we often sit in their deck cabins of an evening & have a yarn. The Doctor is a young Scotsman who has been on the Cape line before, an awfully nice chap, but he has been very seedy since we started, with influenza & is only just getting over it.

Then come the Missionaries, with two exceptions the most unmitigated bounders that ever served behind a counter. They actually can't talk their language grammatically & when one remarked "More didn't I" in answer to " I didn't see it" we simply stared in mute astonishment. One of them missed the ship at the docks. He told us he was in a cab & the cabby wanted to overcharge him sixpence & while he was haggling over it the ship left & he had to go down to the Isle of Wight & get on the pilot boat & after about 10 hours knocking about without any food he was put on the ship at 2 in the morning more dead than alive. He doesn't say whether he bested the cabby for the sixpence but it cost him £3 to catch the ship & the thought of this loss & seasickness have kept him quiet ever since.

The best of the crowd is a man named Leakey,[3] brother of the Cambridge man. He himself has taken his degree & is a very decent sort but of course feels awfully out of it amongst these others....

....My mate Schiff is rather a rowdy youngster with plenty of spirits & I think will turn out a very decent sort. We are in the same cabin & get on famously. He will certainly always be a cheerful companion & is a favourite on the ship. The Captain spoke to me just after we started & asked me if I was fond of Missionaries & as our feelings coincided on that subject he put all their crowd at the lower end of the table & placed Miss Furley & Schiff on his right & Mrs. Fraser & me on his left so we are very comfortable.

At Naples we pick up Lady Alice Portal, wife of the Consul at Zanzibar & a Miss Hardinge.[4] So we shall then be 16 which, with 7 of the officers, makes a fair table full....

....We had service by the skipper this morning & a short sermon by Leakey. This was about 10 minutes utter rot with one tremendous Missionary lie thrown in. However he convinced us all that Bartimeus was blind & a beggar which seemed to me pretty clear before.

Mombasa. June 20th. '92

At last I am anchored again in Africa & from the little I have seen of these parts it is certainly not a patch on the South, though I have had really no opportunity to judge as yet, not having been many miles from the town....

....We arrived off Lamu at nightfall & as it is a very bad harbour, no lights or anything, we had to put to sea again & wait until the next afternoon for the tide. We didn't go ashore as the town is about two miles up the creek, but the next morning, the Chief Officer & I took the boat & went ashore on the North side for a walk & a swim before breakfast which was a great treat. About 10 o'clock several of us went ashore to see Lamu. It is a most extraordinary place. Huge old Portuguese houses of stone with flat stone roofs & most beautifully carved teak doors, jumbled together with native mud-daubed shanties. No streets but just little passages about 3 ft. wide dodging round the houses & in the middle a huge stone fort with heaps of old rusty guns & the Sultan of Zanzibar's[5] red flag flying....

....We sailed out of Lamu in the teeth of a small gale & some fearful squalls of rain & arrived here in Mombasa at 9 o'clock next morning. A lot of the Coy's[6] men came off to meet us & we soon found that grand quarters had been prepared for us with two other chaps, but the skipper asked me to stay on the ship as long as she was in harbour, so I did & enjoyed it.

This place was an awful surprise to me in every way. In the first place there are about 25 employees of the Coy here; Administrator-General, Accountants, Judge, Banker, Post Master, Customs Officers & goodness knows what, and they all appear to be very busy though what they do nobody knows. We are quartered with a Customs Officer & one of the Assistant Accountants, both very decent fellows. The house is a big stone one built just on the edge of the cliff so that we look right down on the harbour. It has a large balcony in front & five large rooms upstairs which we inhabit. Schiff & I have a long narrow room with bedsteads with spring mattresses. There is plenty of ventilation by means of doors & windows which we always keep wide open. We also get a bath every morning & live in the most luxurious style. At 7 o'clock we have a sort of small breakfast, the office hours being from 7:30 to 11a.m. & 1 to 5; just a poached egg & cup of coffee. Then at 11 we have a fish & two or three other courses with beer and at 6:30 p.m. dinner with about 8 courses. Fish of all sorts are very cheap & curried prawns is a staple dish. Since we arrived here I have only dined at home twice & then we had company, so you can imagine we have been pretty lively. H.M.S Blanche came in the same day that we did & there was a general round of festivities. I dined the third night with the A-G (Administrator-General) to meet the Blanche fellows & we had a very jolly evening.

The full dress here is white mess jacket with black trousers, white shirt & coloured cummerbund round the waist. Of course I was not prepared for this sort of things so had to borrow clothes all over the place. I shall be glad when I get away, for this is much too civilized for me.

The town itself is on an island forming the left entrance of the harbour, while about half a mile across on the North is English Point where the

P.W.D.[7] is situated. Here they have extensive workshops & an armoury & as they are always kicking up an awful noise I conclude they do something. Right across the island, about 2 miles South, is Kilindini where the A-G resides in a large double-storey bungalow with armed sentries always patrolling in front. This place is connected with the offices here by telephone & a double lined tramway. They have an engine for the latter but never use it, as each man keeps his own trolley & is pushed out by two natives. They go a rare pace & it is rather good fun on a dark night. The Eastern Telegraph Company office is also at Kilindini and several fellows live there in preference to the town.

The island is covered with dense jungle, baobab & coconut trees & certainly would not be my ideal of a very healthy spot though, beyond severe fits of biliousness, no one seems to have suffered much as yet. The only exercise anyone seems to think of is an occasional game of tennis & as there is only one asphalt court, one can only get about one set in two days for it is dark at six....

....Schiff is getting let down very easily & the fellows all chaff him so much about his high collars & dress that he will soon get out of those ways & once I can get him to work he will find it is not all fun & if I go straight for Uganda, as I hope, we shall have a good march to break him in....

....They talk of abandoning Uganda, in which case we shall most probably have to go up to fetch Capt. Lugard[8] & his troops. The Germans have had an awful licking at Chaga near Kilimanjaro & not far from here, about 150 miles.

Mombasa. July 19th '92

When I last wrote I was suffering from a bilious attack which afterwards turned into my old complaint fever & I had to go to bed for a couple of days, but I soon shook it off & now with plenty of exercise manage to keep more fit.

As I told you, the chief fad of the Coy here has been the laying of the railway,[9] so the other day two of us started over to the mainland on the other side of the island to walk up the line which has been laid for some 8 or 9 miles inland. Of course it is only a small single tram sort of a line but it must have cost a lot of money & labour and as it is never used is going to rack & ruin. After we got to the end of the line we took a small path over the hills to a camp where one of the Coy's men is supposed to be mining for lead. Here we were very well received & he showed us all over the place. The stuff they are working on is certainly of no value in my opinion, but the country round about looks promising & I should have rather liked to have done a few days prospecting there. We had to sleep on stretcher beds without any mattress or blankets but that was nothing as the nights are very warm. The next morning we started back early, taking two natives with us & when we got on to the line we took the first trolley we saw & made them push us. This they are quite used to & by jumping up on the trolley by turns they get rested & take you along at a fine pace. On this trip they took us down the whole 8 miles in 1 & a quarter hours so we had a fine ride & it is awfully exciting work as there are lots of trolleys scattered along on the line, to say nothing of stray sticks, stones &c. So you have to keep a sharp look out & be quick with the brake. We just saved a nasty collision & we ran off once but no one was hurt so it didn't matter.

On my return here I found Schiff in bed with fever but he has not been bad. The fever here is of a much milder type than we had down in the South but S is naturally not very strong & it has pulled him down a bit as he gives in to it too much. I am afraid he will not be fit for marching for a week or so....

....My chief fun here is sailing. I go out nearly every day & on Saturdays & Sundays Mackenzie, the Bank Manager & I, always get off as early as we can & have a little picnic in his boat & have grand times. We have actually made these other chaps so enthusiastic that next Sat. we are going to have a great sailing match for open boats round the island, ten Rupees entrance & there are already six entries. I have chartered a native boat & Mr. Hall's "Frog" looks well on the list. Several fellow who can't sail have given donations & the steam-launch will follow the race with Judges &c., not forgetting life-buoys....

....In the meanwhile I have been worrying up the Public Works Dept. & have got all my saddles, bags &c. completed & have bought 15 donkeys with which I am to make a trial trip as far as Machakos, about half way to Uganda, and there, if I think fit, I can buy as many donkeys as I like from the natives. But I have to wait here for the A-G before starting. I shall only be away about two months from the coast so it will be just a nice little walk.

Mombasa. Aug. 15th '92

These last few days I have been up to my eyes in work getting my expedition ready. But at last everything is done & I only await my written orders & hope to be off myself tomorrow at noon. Schiff, as I think I told you, went to Zanzibar on sick leave so that all the work was left to me. However when the English mail arrived I was ordered to start at once with only the thirty donkeys which I then had, & made all ready when Schiff turned up, so I had to double the rations & make up my mind to take him, though I am afraid he won't go far as his heart is not in the work & he says it is no good working for a failing company. However I have the best authority out here for saying that very shortly the Govt. will take us over & then, as up-country men will stand the best chance of being kept on in the service, I mean to try my level best to make myself as indispensable as possible....

....I am sorry to say that with my usual luck I dropped in for my first funeral in these parts last week. One of the fellows who was not actually in the Coy, but had been previously & was to have conducted the Bishop's caravan up to Uganda, succumbed the other day to acute pneumonia. Of course he was buried next day & with my experience in that line I was made general bosser up of the show. It was a strange sight & very impressive. The grave-yard is at the Mission some two miles down the harbour so we all had to go in boats. The coffin had already been brought down to one of the Customs sheds where it was guarded by four of our native soldiers with fixed bayonets and the Jack for the pall. Six of us carried it down into the boat & the rest of the crowd filled up some six other boats with the Swallow's steam pinnace leading. All flags were half-mast, even the Sultan's on the fort & we steamed slowly down the harbour. When we got to the beach some half mile from the grave we let six natives carry as relief for us as we hadn't a second relief of six able-bodied white men. So we took turn about with the natives but just before reaching the cemetery we took the coffin again and marched slow. The Bishop met us at the gates in full robes & read the service very impressively though he took rather a mean advantage of the occasion, knowing that this was one when we were all present, to give us Coy's. men an awful slating for not attending Church more often (N.B. 50 minute sermons) & drawing a very pointed distinction between us & the men at the Mission. He told us practically that we were doomed & in fact had a special concession in the lower regions where the poor chum we were burying had sort of gone before to peg out the claim. The delivery was too much of the ranting style for me, but his reading was very good & personally he is by far the best man on the Mission. Their caravan starts just after us but I don't think they will see much of us.

    I managed to make up my full complement of donkeys after all by dint of rushing all over the country & sent them off on Thursday to Masera, some twelve miles away, & on Saturday I started Schiff off to go & look after them, while I leave tomorrow in a large dhow with all the loads, boys &c. for a place called Bandarini (close to Rabai) at the extreme end of one of the big creeks running into the mainland from the back of the harbour. Here I pitch my camp for a day or two to get all my packs in order & drill the boys a bit in saddling up & off; & then we go up to Kikuyu, some 90 miles beyond Machakos & about 375 miles from here. I have some splendid donkeys & very cheap as compared to our prices on the fields (£5 to £8). Here mine were an average of Rupees 45, or just under £3 but they are all up-country donkeys & the sooner I get them away from the coast the better....

....The Coy. are reducing their staff here considerably & some 6 to 7 leave by next mail with three months pay in lieu of notice, while many of the up-country stations are to be closed & the men sent home. This looks very bad but I think it is only a ruse to force the hand of the Government. Capt. Smith[10] who has just arrived here as Asst. A-G & is going to take Lugard's place in Uganda, has really come out on Govt. behalf. All stores will be massed at Kikuyu for Uganda & if my donkeys will do alright I shall be running from here to Kikuyu, while Martin,[11] their old caravan hand, will run from there to Uganda. This is the present scheme. Inshallah it will come alright but I would far rather have my job than Martin's with his four hundred porters through Masailand, a hostile country. He has to take most of his men away from here in chains, 6 men chained together by the neck, because they desert before starting. They generally sign on & then they get 3 or 4 months pay in advance to buy anything they want for the road. With this money they go straight for home & have to be brought back & out in chain gang until they are so far up that they can't desert. Thank goodness a chain gang would be no good for me, for 6 men chained by the neck would be little good running after a donkey. So I shall not be bothered with them & my men, who have been used to travelling with a 60 or 70 lb. pack on their heads, will find donkey-wallah business pretty easy & will not feel inclined to desert & get put in a chain gang....

....All my fit out has been immensely admired & everyone has done his best to help & encourage me in my experiment, though of course I have a great deal of prejudice to overcome in the slavery & chain gang way. Our mess gave me a champagne breakfast this morning as a farewell & I am bound to call at the Swallow en passant. So I have a good send-off, & if it can be done it will be a grand success and donkeys will replace human transport....

....My instructions say that if successful I am to establish Stations en route

& run a regular transport to Kikuyu, with Martin working from there to Uganda as I thought. So if the donkeys live I am safe for a good time, but this trip will be a hard one & I have little doubt of its success.

Machakos. Oct. 10th '92

I have had an awful journey up. In fact is was perfectly ridiculous the number of difficulties that cropped up against me. To begin with the country is as dry as a bone; no water & no grass on the road anywhere. Consequently some of the donkeys soon showed signs of fatigue & then one or two died. When we got to Taru,[12] about 50 miles from the coast, we had to cross the plain, nearly sixty miles without water, & as all our donkeys were packed we had no water carrying power. I tried hard to engage natives to carry for us but they were too lazy so I had to make a plan myself. Accordingly, I took 20 donkeys, out of 36 that I had left (4 died), & loaded two with water & every man including myself carried as much as he could. We started one evening & travelled the greater part of the night, off-saddling now & then for a couple of hours until sunrise & then rested all day. In this way I managed the distance in 3 nights....

....I left Schiff in camp with 16 donkeys and 9 men out of the 15, with orders to leave 2 nights after me carrying as much water as he could & I was to send water back 1/3 of the way to meet him. Instead of that he didn't start until the 3rd night & then, being too lazy to pull on all night, tried to make up time in the day, with the consequence that his donkeys arrived in a shocking state & two died almost immediately on their arrival. He himself was very seedy & made the men carry him on his stretcher the greater part of the way which was somewhat rough on the men. He had also thrashed the cook (who was interpreter as well) for some trivial offence & that worthy, with his mate, had run away, so we were left without any interpreter. In fact he made an awful mess of this first attempt at sole charge.

When Schiff arrived he found me in bed with a pretty stiff attack of ague & vomiting & said he was very bad & turned in too. I had a pretty sharp bout which laid me up for 8 days & then the water supply began to run short so it became necessary to shift camp. This we had to do by sections, sending half the donkeys on with loads to the next camp & then they had to return for more. For this stage both Schiff & I rode donkeys as I was unable to walk, but a couple of days in the next camp did me a world of good & as Schiff didn't seem to get any better, & certainly never tried to, I decided to push on, as we had already lost 10 days.

Accordingly we started in the afternoon, & sleeping halfway, reached the next camp 10 miles away the next morning & I managed the march without feeling any fatigue. Schiff of course rode & seemed to get worse instead of better. We had hardly pitched the tent when the Railway Survey caravan came in from Uganda, so of course we went to see them & found them an awfully jolly lot of fellows. Hamilton's friend, Capt. MacDonald,[13] who is in command, was not there as he had been ordered back to Uganda, but I hear he is still at Kikuyu so I shall see him in a day or two. Capt. Smith, our Asst. Administrator Gnl. arrived the same morning so we were a large party & had a very jolly day. In the evening we all dined together at the mess & had a real good feed, for of course these fellows don't forget to live well. Capt. S. had a long consultation with me about Schiff & eventually it was decided the best thing to do was to send him back to the coast. So Smith ordered him back at once & the Ry. Survey fellows promised to see him safe down, so I was left to continue my journey alone. Before this the headman of my boys was sent forward to catch another caravan & get a few more men to help me with the loads, a job which should have taken him 4 days. Instead of which he went visiting friends and only returned the 16th day. So I had to tie him up & give him 25 & dismiss him. So at last I was left alone with 9 men to do the journey and no interpreter. However the men have worked awfully well & I managed to make them understand all I want, so we shove along somehow.

After leaving Tsavo, which is the only real running river in the country, there is a stretch of 55 miles with only two water holes, one at 20 & the other at 30 miles and the last 25 are dry. This was a sore trial for the donkeys with no grass as there was so little water that I could only give them half a bucket each at each place & though I had 32 left at the 2nd hole, I lost six in the following two days & had to leave two behind at the Mission station unfit to travel. I reduced my loads as much as possible & struggled on but they went ahead dying off all along the road, many I believe from sheer exhaustion & I eventually arrived, after innumerable difficulties, three hundred miles from the coast on the 8th with only fifteen donkeys & all my men carrying loads.

From here I have to take an escort of 25 men as we have to pass through a country where there exists a predatory tribe of natives called Masai[14] who have a playful knack of clawing up caravans when they see a chance. I am also taking 34 donkeys from here, besides mine, belonging to the Bishop, & some bullocks. So they would get a nice haul if they succeeded in rushing my camp. However I have 35 guns & plenty of ammunition, so I don't think there is much fear.

Nelson[15] is in charge of Kikuyu & MacDonald is there, so I shall have a good time of it & as there is a plenty of grass & water, my donkeys ought soon to pick up & be ready for the march back. It is only 50 miles from here & by changing donkeys I hope to do it in 3 days.

This place [Machakos] is a grand post, situated right up on the mountains. It is for natives utterly impregnable. The fort is built square & has a six-foot ditch guarded with barbed wire all around. Inside the four sides are houses & stores all around & the centre is prettily laid out with flowers & the flagstaff. The garrison consists of about 50 men who are used as police, despatch runners or porters as occasion requires. They buy a tremendous quantity of food from the natives & store it ready for any passing caravans. The climate is grand; not too hot in the daytime & very cold at night. In fact I find three blankets none too many. The Supt. Ainsworth,[16] who has been on the Congo, is a very decent sort & has made me very welcome & comfortable, & as he has fresh milk & butter galore & fresh vegetables, I have had a good time.

At Kibwezi Mission too, where Dr. Moffat, son of the Matabeleland Moffat & grandson of the Dr. M. is in charge, he made me awfully welcome & insisted on my having all my meals in his place. In fact he is a rattling good chap & we had long chats over South Africa. I will send you one of my maps when I get down to the coast which will give you an idea of my route.

My kit has turned out exactly what I expected & what was wanted & the fellows in Mombasa envied me the expense I had saved by knowing what to get, while they have trunks full of useless clothes &c. which cost a deal of money. My rifle shoots splendidly & I have already killed an antelope & several guinea fowl with it & hope to add to the score tomorrow when I get into game country. One pair of my old boots has already succumbed, the last 25 miles to here being all up the bed of a river through the water &c. which finished them.

Kikuyu. Oct. 22nd '92

You will be surprised to have a letter so soon after my last, but I am stuck for the next ten days at least, so unless I write now I shan't get a letter off to you before Xmas. So though it will be rather previous I must wish you a very Merry Xmas & Happy New Year & many of them. I hope to manage to have my Xmas in Mombasa, but I shall only just get down in time if I do manage it....

....I am off again tomorrow morning to a place about fifteen miles from here to purchase some 8,000 lbs. of food from the natives. The Station has to supply 350 rations for 30 days @ 1 & a half lbs. per diem for the Bishop's caravan to Uganda and we have not enough in store, as Martin's caravan which has just left took 30,000 lbs. So you may imagine it takes some trouble to keep up the supply with such demands....

....Machakos, Kikuyu & Tsavo are the three Stations the company have & they are giving up the last of these, so they will only have the two. The stations are simply used as depots for goods & for buying & supplying passing caravans with food and they have to keep a fairly large garrison (about 100 to 120 men each) for fear of any move on the part of the natives, & as the company is reducing staff & generally economising, there is a chance of their giving up Machakos as well....

....Finding the place [Machakos] too cold & bleak for the donkeys, which were now reduced to 14, I decided to get on, but as the country ahead is infested with Masai, I had to take a strong escort. Ainsworth had 29 donkeys which he had been ordered to buy from the natives and as they were thriving he sent them with me to be looked after at this place, so I had changes for my loads & could travel sharp....

....On reaching the Kiboko, or hippopotamus river, we made a strong kraal & I kept sentries on all night round the camp. One of the men shot a zebra close to camp so they all had a gorge of meat & were very happy.

The next morning we had fifteen miles across the Athi Plains without water, but I did it in one march by changing the loads about & then rested for the remainder of the day. We were now close to the edge of the Kikuyu forest & about 11 & a half miles from the fort so my journey was nearly over. We started at daybreak & following the narrow path through the forest with fine large open glades here & there, we arrived at a small stream which they told me was halfway, so I stopped for half an hour to change donkeys. This part of the road would be a nasty one in a hostile country but fortunately it is a sort of No Man's Land as the Wakikuyu[17] & Masai are deadly enemies, so they are both frightened to go near the forest for fear of ambuscades.

We eventually reached the Fort at Kikuyu at 11 a.m. & I was not sorry the journey was over for it had been one continual fight against obstacles, & even this lengthy description cannot give you an adequate idea of the worry & hard work we had. The men worked cheerfully & willingly all through, & for natives I could not have wished for better, & I shall take good care to keep them permanently in my service. As far as the donkeys experiment goes, the loss on this trip, reckoning every pro & con is only about Rs. 300, or barely £20, so that I am perfectly sure that in an ordinary season, with grass & a better supply of water, it will pay well.

On my arrival here I found Martin's (one of the Coy's) caravan, which had left a fortnight before me for Uganda still waiting for despatches. With him were Major Smith [formerly Captain] who is going to Uganda in Lugard's place; Capt. MacDonald, Hamilton's chum of the Railway Survey; Eugene Wolff, the German traveller & correspondent, & Thompson, Martin's assistant. Nelson is in charge of the Station &. Purkiss, his Lieut., who is also a South African man. So we were 8 Europeans altogether.

The Kikuyu are very treacherous. They have continually worried the Coy's men ever since they arrived. To begin with they attacked & burnt the first station the Coy. built near here. Then on another occasion they attacked a caravan that was carrying up a steel boat in sections & wrecked the lot. Then, not many months ago, they murdered the mail men (3) & destroyed the mails & it is quite a common occurrence for them to cut a man off when he is out to fetch wood or water & kill him just for fun.

Machakos. Nov. 14th 1892

I have reached this far on my way back & leave first thing tomorrow for Mombasa. Fortunately, I have a lot of time expired, men from here & Kikuyu, so have a large caravan, about 80 men all told with 30 rifles, and I hope to get through without molestation....

....I have been collecting a few curios which I shall send by the next mail; spears, arrows &c. I am taking from here about 20 porter loads of 65 lbs. each of curios for Capt. MacDonald, Major S. & others. In fact it is a regular curio caravan. This will be my first attempt to take a body of men any distance & as we have to travel nearly 15 days without any chance of buying food, it requires a little management. The rains have commenced up here so I hope I shall not have the same difficulty with water as I had coming up....

....Poor Mackenzie the banker, my great chum in Mombasa, is dead from fever. Schiff has gone home still seedy, MacDonald gone to Uganda to make enquiry for Govt. into the late rows.

Mombasa. Dec. 7th '92

I received your letter on the road about two days from here & I have just managed by hard marching to catch this mail, though it starts in a few hours, so I shall not have time to write very much.

I have had a splendid trip down & as I was carrying the mails did some record marching. From Machakos to the coast, 300 miles, I marched in 17 days, an average of nearly 18 miles a day which is reckoned good for these parts. I should have done it in less but had to delay one day to buy food for the men as most of their food has been spoilt by the rain....

....I have been awfully busy here paying off the men & had to write a short report to the Directors for this mail, my full report to go in by next. The experiment has not been a success this time as nearly all the donkeys died, but what could be expected in such a fearfully dry season. No animal can travel without food and water. Coming down I had to bring all the sick, lame & lazy from the different stations, about 100 men, so I travelled more comfortably than on the road up as I had heaps of servants & after I had had a few of them well flogged for misdemeanours they gave me very little trouble.

I arrived just in time for another boat race on Saturday afternoon & of course entered the same boat "Frog". It was a glorious success. Fifteen boats started & we sailed right round the island, about 12 miles. There is a cable ship here & the officers entered 4 boats & in addition there were two steam launches in attendance. It was an awfully pretty sight as the boats all kept well together & it was great fun chaffing each other as we passed on different tacks. I jumped into third place soon after the start & later went on up to second but unluckily got into a current when out in the open sea just before the run in for home & I only came fourth, however better luck next time. The Frog is a splendid little boat, though native built, but we have all put on such huge sails now that we have to be pretty careful or over we go.

I managed to keep clear of the fever all the way down by taking 10 grains of quinine every day & I intend to keep it up as long as I am here.

My great chum Victor Mackenzie died here while I was away & I feel somewhat lost without him. I have taken up my quarters in the old house & am very comfortable. Schiff ought to be at home by this time; he has written to me once or twice and says he will write again from home. I must write to his father but have not time this mail.

Our fruit season is just on now & I am enjoying the pineapples immensely.

We have any amount of bananas, oranges, pineapples &c. they are very cheap, about 4 pice not quite a penny for a pineapple, so you may imagine I do eat just a few....

....I haven't any idea yet how long I shall have to stay here or what my next move will be but I hope to get away soon & get back to Kikuyu....

....I had a splendid bit of sport on my way down when I shot my first giraffe. I broke his leg with my second shot at long range as he ran across the road in front of me, & then off I started with two men as hard as we could run but the brute lolloped along on three legs a jolly sight faster than we could go & if he hadn't stopped to look at us every quarter of a mile or so we should have seen nothing more of him. As it was we managed to keep pretty well up to him for about two miles & then we lost him in the bush but I wouldn't give it up. So we took up the spoor and after about three quarters of an hour tracking through very bad ground we came on him suddenly in an open space. My dog "Shetani"[18] had just come up after a long chase behind the rest of the giraffes, there were 9 altogether, & he rushed at the beast but could not make it out at all, however I got another shot in along his spine & he half turned which enabled me to get one in the shoulders & down he came like a house falling, the dog nearly getting squashed under him. It was a perfect bit of sport & I was delighted to get him after our long chase. He was a grand beast, just over 13 ft from head to foot & as fat as a pig. Worst luck he had run straight away from the camp & we found ourselves with about 70 lbs. each & I carried the shin bones, tongues & tail & a jolly heavy load it was. I was very glad to get in. I took the tongue &c. on to Dr. Moffat's next day & we had a glorious dinner together. I took a large piece of the skin too as a trophy for a mat but this & the tail were both spoilt as I could not cure them for it rained incessantly for four days afterwards.

Mombasa. 28. 12. 92

I have been very busy during my spare time in writing an official Report of my journey & my pains have so far been rewarded by the A-G telling me it was a most interesting document. I managed to cover 12 pages of foolscap, so you may imagine it was no slight undertaking for me.

I am still here virtually on leave, no one bothers me & I can do as I like. The A-G said I must require a holiday after my trip & of course I didn't refuse, but I hope they will send me off again shortly....

....Berkeley[19] is leaving the Coy's service, he gave us a farewell dinner on

Xmas Eve which was a great affair, 22 Coy's men sat down & we had a glorious night. We are all awfully sorry that Berkeley is going, he is a grand fellow. We are going to give him a piece of plate. Our new A-G Piggott[20] is a very nice fellow but nothing to compare with Berkeley.

Notes

1. Jack Le Fleming (1868-1943), Francis Hall's brother-in-law who married Hall's sister Ethel.

2. Church Missionary Society.

3. Canon R.H. (Harry) Leakey (1868-1940). Born in Le Havre and educated at Reading, Peterhouse and Ridley Hall, Cambridge. He devoted his life to missionary work among the Kikuyu and lived at Kabete where he translated the Bible into Kikuyu.

4. The daughter of Mr. A. Hardinge, later Sir Arthur Hardinge, Her Majesty's Agent at Zanzibar.

5. Seyyid Hamed-bin-Thwain.

6. The Imperial British East Africa Company (IBEA) was usually referred to as the Company.

7. Public Works Department.

8. Frederick Dealtry Lugard (later Lord Lugard). Colonial administrator and Empire builder. Recruited by IBEA in 1889, he was sent to find a route from Mombasa to the Company's station at Machakos bypassing the Taru desert. In August 1890 he led an expedition to Uganda to establish a British presence and to negotiate a treaty with Mwanga, the Kabaka or ruler of Uganda.

9. The absurdly optimistic 24 inch gauge railway line which extended inland from Mombasa for all of seven miles and was known as The Central Africa Railway. "It was never more than a gesture of good intention and, only once was it used for any purpose more practical than a picnic." Permanent Way, M.F. Hill. Vol 1 p 48.

10. Captain Eric Smith (Later Major), 1st Life Guards. Designed, built and named Fort Smith at Kikuyu with the help of his assistant Mr. Purkiss. Lost an arm in action in Sudan.

11. James Martin was an illiterate Maltese sailor, baptised as Antonio Martini, who first reached East Africa in an American ship when her skipper ran aground off Zanzibar. He accompanied the explorer Joseph Thomson on his famous expedition across Masailand to Lake Victoria in 1883. Later he was second-in-command of the Sultan of Zanzibar's troops and became a well known caravan leader for the IBEA. Despite his illiteracy, Martin rose to the rank of District Commissioner in the East Africa Protectorate administration. F.J. Jackson (later Sir Frederick) taught Martin to sign his name and he used to disguise his inability to write by pretending to have bad eyesight. His correspondence was written for him by a Goanese cousin, da Silva. Martin was recognized as an able administrator, though he may have been the target of Sir Clement Hill's remark that administration in Kenya would suffer "as long as Civil Servants were enlisted from the gutter."

12. Taru desert.

13. Captain J.R.L. Macdonald, leader of the 389 man survey party for the proposed Uganda Railway from Mombasa to Lake Victoria.

14. A tall, slim, handsome tribe of Nilo-Hamitic origin, the Maasai enjoyed the reputation for being the most warlike, rapacious and disciplined tribe in East Africa. Their warriors, known collectively as Elmoran, were famous for their powers of endurance and peerless fighting qualities in open country. Lion hunting with spears and cattle raids were the chief occupations of the day, and since they believed that God originally gave all the cattle in the world to the Masai, felt themselves innocent of any crime. The Masai were greatly feared by their Bantu neighbours and early British colonialists admired their pride, courage and independence.

15. E. Nelson. Administrative officer, Kikuyu District.

16. John Ainsworth. Joined IBEA in 1888 and was their representative in Machakos.

17. Usually referred to as the Kikuyu, they were a mainly forest dwelling Bantu tribe with an intricate clan system and an iron age culture. Occupying steeply-ridged fertile highlands extending from Mount Kenya to the Nairobi River, the hard working women were skilful agriculturists. The Kikuyu people were jealous of their territory and resisted the invading white men by all means available. This may account for one colonial officer's description of them in the 1890's as "undoubtedly a treacherous, untrustworthy crowd," and an early missionary's opinion of them as "distrustful and suspicious with a tendency to dissimulation and guile."

18. Kiswahili for Satan.

19. E.J. L. Berkeley, (later Sir Ernest). Went to Uganda with the British Mission in 1893, became Commissioner of Uganda in 1895 and was reappointed, after a short absence, in 1898.

20. J.R.W. Pigott, Administrator General IBEA. Led an expedition to the Tana Valley and assisted Professor J.W. Gregory's scientific safari in 1892. Later appointed to the East Africa administration.

Map 3 Kenya coast and hinterland

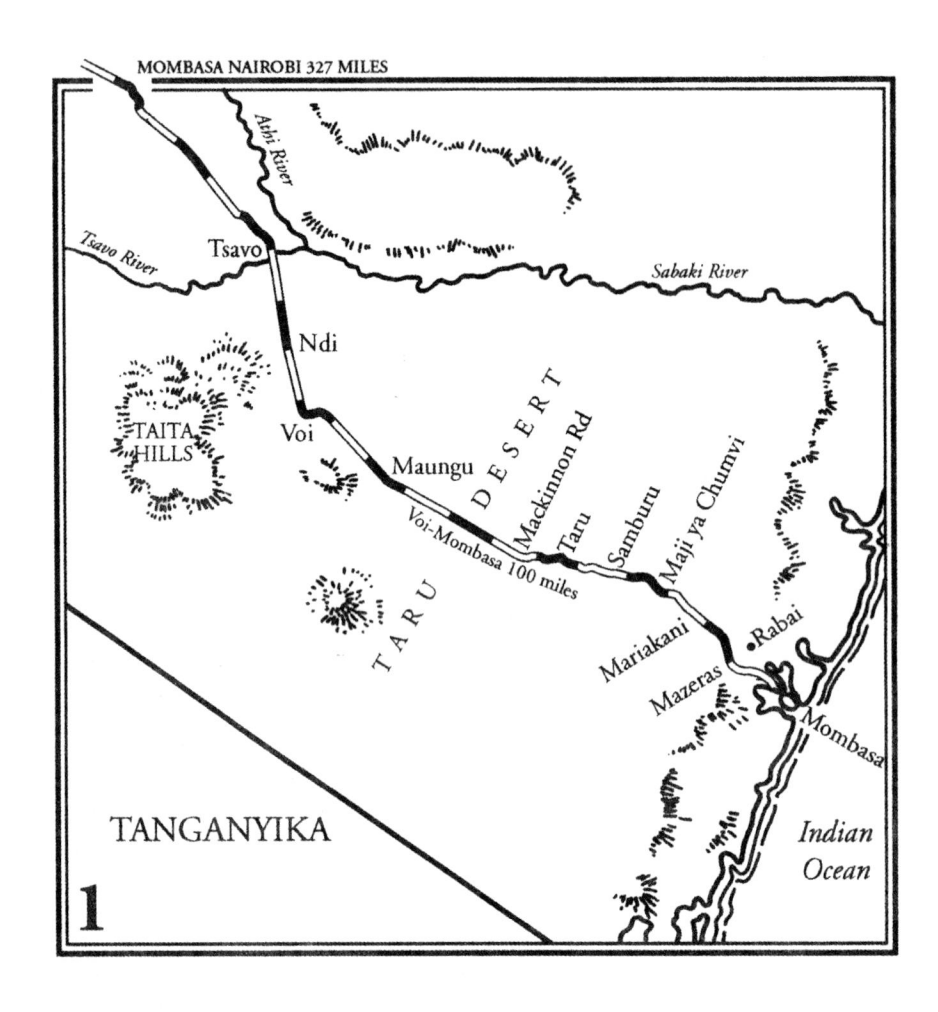

Chapter 2

MAKING FRIENDS IN KIKUYULAND

Mombasa. Jany. 25th 1893

Since my last I have had some funny experiences & a bit of a change from my caravan work. Pending the answer of our Directors to my report, our new A-G decided I ought to be made some use of, so the first job they gave me was to take stock of a ship. Of course I knew nothing about the job but that didn't matter. I got a trip to Zanzibar free & had a real good time....
....Returning in the ship was Lieut. Villiers of the Horse Guards who wanted to catch up Portal's[1] caravan as he was to go with them to Uganda. So immediately we arrived I was ordered to pilot him up the road. We landed at 7.30 a.m. and by 2 p.m. I had porters & all ready & we left in the steam launch at 3 p.m. Landing at the first camp, about twelve miles up the creek, we marched straight away & halted at 1 in the morning. At 6.30 we were on the road again & by dint of marching all day we reached their camp, 35 miles march, at 5 p.m., not a bad bit of work. Unfortunately we got wet & then dried by the sun so I suffered a slight touch of fever but it only lasted a day.

Our Supt. of Transport is very ill poor chap, so the next job they put me on was to assist him & now he has got so bad that he can't come to the office. I have to run the whole show & also have charge of the General Stores, so I have my hands full & it is positively beastly work as I have to take stock & be at the desk all day. I shall be delighted when I get marching orders.

Poor old Nelson died of dysentery at Kikuyu on 26th Dec. It was a great blow to me, he was such a great chum of mine.

I have had no time to pack all my curios but by this mail I am sending Min^2 a few pieces of Lamu China, very rare & supposed to be valuable. There is a history attached to it but I have never been able to hear much of it beyond the fact that three shiploads reached Africa some 400 years ago & the Arabs value it highly. I had this lot given me by a lady who is leaving for Bombay as a parting present and as a sort of commission, for I acted as auctioneer for them & got grand prices for all the furniture. Her husband has been constructing the telegraph wire for the company, & as it is finished up the coast to Lamu, he is leaving....

....Villiers gave me a lovely little detective camera in a leather case all complete & I am just studying photography & I shall now be able to send some photos of scenes &c. on my travels, though I don't think I shall trouble to develop them myself as I can get it done better at home.

Mombasa. Feb. '93

At Kikuyu, where I hope to be in about 30 days, Purkiss had been besieged for 6 days but Portal's crowd turned up in time to clear things up, but he lost ten killed & two wounded....

....I have had a wretched time here lately, having to look after two Departments & stick to office hours (approximately) but I am glad to say I have got my marching orders for Kikuyu & I start tomorrow. It is an awful rush as I have to arrange for 120 men's rations for the road, all the loads, pack my kit & everything just on mail day & I haven't had any time for letters in the office. I got an awful slating from the Directors for "utterly ignoring" all orders issued by them on my last trip but this is scarcely to be wondered at as I never saw or heard of them before, & the written orders given me by Major Smith are totally different from those of the Directors, so that he also knew nothing of them....

....My orders now are to go to Kikuyu & assist Purkiss pro. tem. & use my spare time in making a wagon track down as far as Kibwezi to meet the Mission road; & to train cattle, donkeys &c. for transport & look after everything on that section of the road; about as nice a job as I could wish for as I am to have as free a hand as possible. This will probably keep me up-country for the rest of my three years & I ought to have a real good time, for the work is none too hard. I think, if it is not too expensive, I should like to have some good newspapers regularly while up there as we get so fearfully behind the world without them. The Weekly "Penny Graphic" is not common here & I think I should like it best but anything will do....

....By this mail I am sending a case of curios & a bundle of spears....The big long-bladed spear is a Masai spear, used for stabbing only; the next two broadest are Wa-Kikuyu spears, & the four with a sharp ridge in the blade are Somali. All these are native iron & native made & Masai spears especially are valued greatly amongst natives as a Masai rarely parts with his spear until he is killed.

Kikuyu. April 2nd '93

Here I am back again in my old quarters & I hope they will leave me with a free hand for the rest of my term of service. I shall have plenty to do for the whole of that time as I have about 150 miles of road to make besides the transport work. The station here seems strange with poor old Nelson gone but Purkiss who is now in charge is a splendid fellow & also an old South African so we have lots of notions in common & get on splendidly together. We intend to put in all the work we can before Portal's return to make a good show, for should the Government take over, which seems pretty certain will be the case, we must do our best to ensure obtaining a Govt. billet. I think we stand a good chance & I for one shall make a point of trying hard for it. We are making carts & are going to train bullocks & donkeys as well as make the road, so we shall have plenty to do, but it is beautifully cool up here so we can manage to do some work in comparative comfort.

I did a pretty fair journey up from the coast, 32 days, of which I was actually marching 28, not bad considering the men each carry 65 lb. loads on their heads besides their kit. As far as the Scottish Mission at Kibwezi, 200 miles, I had the company of the new Doctor Supt. [Charters] & a professional gardener who came out with him, so the loneliness of the journey was relieved for the greater part of the way. Thank goodness there was plenty of water on the road so we had no trouble on that score & got along very comfortably. I had the usual troubles with the porters on starting, several desertions &c. though not so many as usual. The Company put a premium on desertion by paying the men two months wages in advance so of course if they can get away they will & sometimes it is hard to catch one, but when he is caught he gets it pretty hot....

....I had a few adventures on the way & novel experiences at Maungu Camp. I was sitting under a big tree having a cup of tea with Dr. Charters when a long green tree snake let himself down on to my hand. The tea which I was holding of course went all over the Doctor & myself & the snake made off but one of the men killed him before he got very far. It was a harmless snake but we hadn't time to investigate this matter before his death....

....I had a perfectly grand sight of Kilimanjaro.[3] The rain of the night before had evidently turned to snow there & the whole mountain, as low down as one could see from that distance of about 100 miles, was covered with snow which glistened beautifully in the rising sunlight. It is not often seen so completely covered, so I was lucky, & it appeared so close that one could hardly realise it was really so far off....

....I had a very jolly two days stay at Machakos, giving my men a rest, and then went on. I found the Athi River full and impassable but as I had intended to have a day's shooting here it was no great drawback. I had no luck for the greater part of the day but in the afternoon, returning up the river, I made a snap shot at a hippopotamus in the water &, putting in a neat shot just behind the ear, settled him. He kicked round for a few minutes & then sank, & as they don't rise for some hours, I returned to camp which we reached after dark.

The next morning I was off early with my boy & ordered fifteen men to follow, going to the place where I had shot him. We went on three quarters of a mile down the river when my boy touched me & I saw two lions swimming the river in front, about 200 yds off. I rushed on and arrived at the top of the bank just in time to see a fine lion landing within 30 yds of me. The moment he caught sight of us he let out the most awful roar & made a bound towards us. This fairly frightened me for I thought, if I can't stop him first shot I'm done. So I thought it better to leave him alone & he turned & made off like light, for which I was devoutly thankful. The lioness in the meanwhile had turned & was swimming for the opposite bank. I waited until she crawled out onto the bank & then let go. I hit her too far back in the body for she just dropped for a moment & then got up & crawled off, & as the river was very full of both water and alligators,[4] I didn't attempt the crossing to follow her. I found my hippo close by & no doubt this is what they were after. The men arrived just afterwards & we spent the greater part of the day hauling out &

cutting up the meat & there was great joy in the camp that night....

....The rains were awful & the passage through the Kikuyu bush was like swimming in a thunderstorm but by this time I was thoroughly accustomed to it & I reached here all well. It was a treat to sleep in a house & know that you hadn't got to march next morning. Purkiss is going down to the Athi for a few days' shooting so I shall be alone, but I have plenty to do so shall not feel it....

....When next you write I should be awfully glad to get a parcel of newspapers. Anything will do as long as it is something to read, as I shall probably by that time be all alone in camp somewhere on the road & have a good few hours to pass away. I have made all arrangements at the coast to have letters &c. forwarded so I am sure of getting them, barring the Masai....

....We have any number of cattle here now, captured from the natives, so we have our own butter, milk & everything & it is very like living on a farm in the colony, & with a flock of 250 goats & sheep we are not likely to run out of meat. In fact the place is a perfect paradise after Mombasa, & if they will only leave me in peace to do my work I don't want to see the coast again until I am on my way home.

Kikuyu. May 1st '93

We have been getting an awful dose of rain since I arrived here. It commenced first on the 11th March & up to yesterday we had registered by gauge 24 inches. Last night there was nearly an inch & a quarter & it has poured the greater part of the day. It is enough to give anyone the jim-jams.

As for work it is perfect misery. I get wet through every day & the poor beggars of men have an awful time of it. In fact if it keeps on like this I shall stop the work till the weather breaks.

I think I told you that I have to make a road from here to Machakos, thence to Kibwezi. I started this about a fortnight ago having taken a rough survey of the best line of country. Commencing with only 30 men I have now got 50 on, besides some of the wily natives of the District, to clear the jungle & scrub ahead of the main party. It would astonish people at home to see us going to work. All the men with their rifles in one hand & their tools in the other, & while at work the gangs keep close together with their rifles piled on either side while one or two guards are always walking backwards & forwards. When I go on a few hundred yards ahead to put in the flags, two armed men follow me, & I of course always carry my revolver handy. These men are so treacherous & have played so many dirty tricks before, that we give them no chance now in spite of their apparent friendliness. But it is an awful nuisance as we have also to take up our flags & lines every night or we should never see them again....

....Once outside the bush there is no further trouble as far as Machakos except the drifts. I have already completed the first two miles & am now at the easy part down the ridge. We get out at 8 in the morning, taking food, an hour for lunch & back at 4 p.m.....

....By the bye, in your letter you confuse Kikuyu & Dagoreti which is hardly to be wondered at, for none of the maps gives any idea of the places. Kikuyu is really the name of the District which extends from the Kapiti Plains on the S.E., Ngongo Bagase[5] S.W., & Kenia Mt. & nearly up to the Aberdare Range on the N. & N.E. Dagoreti was the Coy's Station at a place about 3 miles from here which was captured and burnt by the natives some two years ago. Major Smith was then sent up to rebuild the Station, but preferring this spot, built this fort which is called Fort Smith, Kikuyu, but more generally Kikuyu. It is the only Station the Coy. has in the District & is the most advanced post or depot for supplies on the road to Uganda....

....My poor old dog Shetani died about a fortnight after getting here in spite of all endeavours to save him. I felt as if I had lost an old friend....

....We had a chap Gregory[6] here the other day from the British Museum on Geological and Natural History discoveries & it seemed awfully funny to hear him asking about the state of the ice & snow on Mt. Kenia which he hopes to ascend. We can see the snow-crowned peak of Mt. Kenia on clear days though it is a long way off. Gregory has only 40 men with him & it is a dangerous part for Masai, so we rather expect to see the remains of his party turn up here again one of these days....

....I have made a cart here on some wheels which I brought up with me & intend to use it for shifting camp &c. on the road & am trying hard to get a wagon, but the Coy. is going very slow until they know how things are going in Uganda. Col. Rhodes[7] advised me to worry them until I got it, for he agreed with me that it was a waste of time & money working with porters or even pack animals. Did Ted[8] know him in Bombay? I took a great fancy to him & he was certainly the most practical of all that crowd. And now I must get off to bed as I have to solder up a tin of pickled reptiles & pack a case for Gregory tomorrow to go to the coast & the men leave early.

Kikuyu. May 28th '93

I shifted camp to a spot about 4 miles from the Fort on the 18th so as to be closer to the work. I took 40 men for the road work & 10 to do camp guard night & day & altogether I have 32 guns. I made a jolly camp on a big ridge about 150 yds. from the water with a hundred yards clear space all round as I had to reckon on the chances of attack. Of course the forest stretches pretty well all round, but from the door of my tent I have a lovely view right over the forest & across the Athi Plains to a mountain called "Doinyu Sabuk" in the East....

....I have been getting on splendidly with all the Chiefs along the road & have had no trouble or disputes the whole way. I have had to cut through standing crops, & what is worse in their ideas, to cut down heavy timber & bush which they use to form a barrier round their kraals against Masai attacks. I have managed to avoid actually going through their kraals. Thank goodness I have finished about 5 miles of the road & have at last cleared out of the cultivated portion & have only the forest ahead of me.

The last two or three days there seems to have been some trouble in the wind as some of the neighbouring chiefs stopped their people bringing food, always their first step, & Purkiss had to bring one of them to book & make him come in to explain. This he did & apologised, gave a present & swore eternal friendship in their usual lying way....

....The great event of the month has been the arrival here, en route for the coast, of Capt. Williams[9] & Major Smith from Uganda with about 600 men. The company evacuated on 31st March & Sir Gerald [Portal] took over temporarily (for 12 months) on behalf of Govt. Captain MacDonald is Chief in Command up there & the remainder of Portal's staff, with the exception of Col. Rhodes, remains there until further orders....

....Williams was very much struck with Kikuyu & said, as Portal did, that it was the only place in the country in which there seemed to be any work done. The crops & gardens are looking splendid & both of them simply gorged themselves with the good food while they were here....

....Our friendly chiefs have been away all day but at sundown we saw a fire about a mile away on the road & some time after dark they came in with emissaries from the malcontents bringing the food & sheep demanded & professing a sincere desire for friendship & peace....Of course we had to have a long palaver in which they told me as many lies as they could crowd into the space of time and today (Wednesday) we had to eat with them the liver, kidney &c. of the sheep to seal the compact. Their custom is to eat it raw but we insisted on warming it a bit in a pan. As this is about the 25th time that this ceremony has been performed in the two years that P. has been here, we know what value to put on it.

Kikuyu. June 24th '93

I am now clear of the Wakikuyu pro. tem. & am camped on the Nairobi River, 10 miles from the Fort & just on the edge of the Kapiti Plains....
....At present hyaenas are the great curse. There are literally swarms of them & they are awfully cheeky. The other night there was a great hubbub & I made sure the Masai were on us, but rushing out with my rifle I was just in time to see a man extricating himself from his tent which had come down about his ears. A hyaena had come right into his tent after some meat & had collared his leg. The sentry rushing to the rescue belaboured both man & beast with the butt of his rifle through the tent & the result was general confusion during which the beast made off. The man was more frightened than hurt but he sat by a huge fire & moaned & groaned for the rest of the night. I always shoot these brutes if I see them in daytime but it does not seem to keep them away.

After our long spell without letters we got two mails within 3 days....The papers were very acceptable & are now at Machakos, Purkiss & I having read them. You needn't bother what kind of papers to send; anything is acceptable as we are pretty hard up for reading matter. Ainsworth always sends us all his to read & we send all we get to him when we have read them. The last lot he sent consisted chiefly of "The Times" daily & I have waded through every word of each; market reports, advertisements & all, so you may imagine we read anything. As for the Home Rule debate I have read so much of it that I really begin to get quite interested. The best settlement that I can see is to exile old Gladstone to Ireland & pray for his speedy death....
....Kibwezi, the East African Scottish Mission St., to which spot I am supposed to complete my road, is 210 miles from Mombasa & 140 from Kikuyu, between the River Tsavo & Nzowi Mtn., both of which you will probably find on your map. You see I have a pretty long job ahead of me, though I have completed the worst 10 miles on the route....
....I am now on the edge of the Kapiti Plains, the finest bit of game country in the territory, & though I shall be more in the thick of it when I get to the Athi River, about 12 miles further, I can't grumble at the last 10 days' sport....

....I was hard at work on Saturday but on Sunday 18th, a red letter day for me, I sallied out about noon with two men, one of whom was armed with a Snider (I generally take one or two to send back for the porters if I kill anything) & I of course carried my little sporting Martini....

....While pursuing [a Thomson's gazelle] I found myself close to some wildebeeste so I let the Thomsonii go & started a crawl for the bigger game. Getting a shot at one at 200 yds. I fired & down he went, but got up again & began staggering along on three legs. I rushed up towards him & what was my surprise at seeing a yellow looking animal, which in the long grass looked like a calf, jump up between me & the wildebeeste & go lolloping after him. In a minute he was up to him & sprang on his back & then I grasped the fact that it was a lion. A short sharp fight ensued which was a magnificent sight, but the wildebeeste was soon done & the lion crouched on top of him looking at me as if to dare me to dispute possession. I had only two cartridges left & as it was bare open veldt, not a tree for miles & no cover but the grass, there was no chance of escape if he charged. However there was no time to think of chances. Calling the man to come up handy with his gun, in case my two shots were not sufficient, I walked up slowly to within 50 yds. & his majesty started to slink off slowly, offering me a good broadside, though keeping his head turned to watch me carefully. I fired at his shoulder, hitting rather high on the spine & bowled him over. He then crouched down with his head wagging about & looked rather nasty so I put in my second shot, hitting him again in the spine & the bullet lodged just at the back of the skull. This flattened him out but as I could not see him well in the long grass I took the man's gun & gave him another just to make sure before approaching. But we found the second shot had finished him; in fact either of the first two would have been fatal. I was delighted. I let out such a yell that the men who had come to fetch the ostrich about a mile off came rushing up & they were all as pleased as I was. It was a sight to do the heart of any shootist good; to see the lion & the wildebeeste lying within 6 yds. of each other, both grand specimens of their kind, both full grown males & each bearing traces of their recent combat. The whole thing was a very tragic affair but nothing like you read in books. The lion gave none of those gigantic leaps & bounds (except the one to spring on to the wildebeeste's back). He went along at a clumsy lolloping canter exactly like a calf. There was not a whimper out of either animal during the fight, though they rolled over & over, & the lion never uttered a sound, even after he was wounded. The greatest compliment I had, though all the men congratulated me, was from one of the Wakikuyu who had come out with the men. He said he must go back at once & tell his people, "because it was no good for them to go against a white man, while I with my little gun could kill a lion & a wildebeeste together." They will be more frightened of us now which is perhaps a good thing.

As for the men they look on my little rifle now as a sort of supernatural weapon & they frequently ask how such a little gun sends the bullets so far and kills such big things. The lion is full grown with tawny mane & the skin measures 9' 9" from tip to tip & is in perfect condition. So I shall have one trophy worth sending you when I go to Mombasa next & I can pride myself on the fact of having shot my first lion in fair & open field....

....My little rifle is just perfection & I only want to kill a rhino now to prove that it is good enough to kill anything. It has more than paid for itself over & over in meat & ostrich feathers....

....I find my road from the Fort to this river by cyclometer 10 miles 490 yards. The old road was 11 so I have gained a good bit. A few days ago I went out to try for some fresh meat to send Purkiss as there were some porters passing from Machakos. I wounded a wildebeeste which of course must needs run straight away from camp & took me further than I intended to travel, & then the brute met a chum & having warned him, promptly laid down & died. So I shot his chum alongside him for revenge. I was cutting up these with 14 men, only 4 of whom had guns, when I saw a huge mob of natives like a swarm of ants coming down a valley on our right in a direction that would cut off any hope of retreat to the camp. Of course I made sure they were Masai on the warpath & it gave me a bit of a fright. There was no hope of bolting from such a swarm on the open plains & my fellows simply quaked with fear & would have tried a bolt, but I swore I would shoot everyone of them if they did, & with the respect they have for my little rifle they thought they had better risk the natives. There was nothing for it but to put a bold face on it. So telling the men to go on cutting up, I took a man who could talk Masai & advanced towards the leaders. Three men came forward & what was my delight to find they were Wakamba[10] from Machakos who had been to fight the Masai but had not found any. These fellows were very friendly so I gave the Chief some meat & then divided half a beast into portions & the frantic scrambles for the meat were most ludicrous. Their food was all done & they were nearly starving. There were about 1000 or 1200 of them, though only a few dozen turned off their road to come to us. I was very pleased the episode ended satisfactorily to all concerned.

Athi River. Aug. 2nd '93

Since I last wrote, Berkeley, our former A-G who went to Uganda as Asst. Commr. under Portal, has returned and is now on his way home with final reports &c. of the Commission. I was camped about 9 miles from here when he passed &, as he couldn't stop the night with me (he was going forced marches to catch the French Mail at Zanzibar) he asked me to come on to this camp & dine with him & have a chat. This I was only too delighted to do for more reasons than one, for I had not seen a white man nor spoken my own lingo to anyone for a month. So after we had lunched & he had rested a bit, I sent off 4 of my men with my tent, bedding &c. and we jogged on together.... .

....Berkeley & I had a very jolly evening together & he told me all the news he could about Uganda affairs, though of course he couldn't divulge everything. He expects to reach home by the end of August & thinks it will be about the end of October or November before we shall know definitely what the Govt. intend to do. However he told me not to worry my head about my billet, as us up-country fellows would be sure to be wanted....

....All our fellows in the offices at the coast are feeling very anxious & I am afraid most of them will get their walking tickets if the Govt. take over. This would be a cruel blow for some who only get Rs.200 a month which barely keeps them. The luxurious lazy habits of a tropical life, where one has a servant to do everything for one, are not good training for a struggling junior clerk in a Glasgow merchant's office, whence most of them originally started. They are an awfully good lot of chaps & I should be awfully sorry if they were sacked....

....I have shot up to date 37 head including 3 lions, 1 rhino, 1 hippo, 4 ostriches, 12 wildebeeste, 4 zebra, 4 hartebeeste, 5 Grantii, 2 Thomsonii, 1 alligator & innumerable hyaenas, so that I can't grumble at want of sport for this last six weeks anyway. Many wealthy men in England would pay a lot of money to get the same. The amount of ground I must have covered during this time must be tremendous. However it keeps me in perfect health; I am as hard as nails now. The curse in this camp are the ticks in the long grass. I thought I had seen a few before in some parts of the South but this licks creation. When I come in of an evening my boy scrapes them off my clothes with my sheath-knife & when I undress to go to bed it takes me about 10 minutes or more to pick them all off my body, & as the beasts generally leave their heads behind, one's whole body is in a continual state of irritation. The men suffer just as much & many of them look as if they had had smallpox from continually scratching.

Kikuyu. Aug. 29th '93.

Since I last wrote, events have been occurring somewhat rapidly, that is for Africa, and I'm glad to say that I think very favourably for me. Purkiss has long been promised a billet in Uganda, & when Berkeley came down he was told he might go up at once if he liked. However Berkeley had said nothing about it to the Company so Purkiss could not go. However he sent in his resignation, & as Major Smith was going up with a large caravan, decided to leave with him without further ado. As the nearest available Coy's officer, I of course had to take charge of the Station pending further orders. Fortunately these orders arrived before Purkiss left & I was curtly instructed to take charge at once. So here I am, stuck for goodness knows how long as Acting Supt. of the Post & District.

I had left here on the 9th. & went to Machakos to go on with the road-making from that end, but Major Smith arrived there the day after & he advised me to return with him as he had a good notion of what was going to happen. We reached here again on the 19th. & found Gedge,[11] (The Times Special) had already arrived from Uganda & Sir Gerald Portal & Col. Rhodes came in about an hour later. So we had a great gathering, the biggest yet on record for the Station, 7 Europeans & about 1100 men. They all stayed here for a week & we had a very jolly time though of course there was plenty of work to do.

Some idea of what is expected at this Station may be had from the fact that we not only had to supply food for all hands for the week, but Smith's 630 men required 25 days' food in addition for the road, Gedge's 60 men 4 days' food, & 130 Nubians[12] left here, as well as the garrison of 150, a pretty large order. All hands here get beads for rations & with these can buy any amount of food from the natives & we served out over 20,000 lbs. wt. of grain for the road as it is impossible to buy food on the road from here to Uganda, for 25 days' march.

It was very difficult to get anything out of Portal as to future plans, but Col. Rhodes told us the general plan. The Govt. will send Imperial Service men to command these Forts (Machakos & Kikuyu). Major Smith & Purkiss are to build another at once at Sio Bay, the N.E. corner of Nyanza, whence goods will be sent by boat to Port Alice (Uganda). A new Station is to be built 10 days march from here, North West on Mau plateau, & the Administration of the interior will be stationed either there or here.

Grades of officers, 1st Class £650, 2nd Class £450, 3rd Class £250, with allowance for servants & food & £50 per annum extra for each language. Besides these there will be the office & store clerks.

We fellows who get into the service, & from what they said us up-country fellows are sure of it, start as Third Class Assistants & shall be allowed our £50 a year for Swahili[13] from the start if we pass the exam, which I don't think there is much trouble in doing. So that with £300 a year and allowances in a place like this, we ought to be able to save a fair sum. I am afraid it will mean 3 years service & 6 mos. leave but this does not seem to have been decided.

Portal is going to stay in England about a month & if things are satisfactory will return as far as here to set everything going. I should not be surprised to get orders from him when he reaches the coast to hoist the Union Jack here at once. He said that this Station would never have less than 3 Europeans so it will be very jolly, but in the meanwhile I have to sit in solitude & await the course of events.

I am very lucky in getting this Station just now. In fact had I arranged it all myself it could not have turned out better. I have a very good Goanese clerk who has been here nearly two years, & as the men know me very well, everything goes on as smoothly as possible.

The native headmen (15 of them) came in when we sent for them & said farewell to Purkiss & professed the greatest friendship for me, & after much chin wagging departed. Since then they continue dropping in by ones & twos for the inevitable baksheesh & I really think they begin to think it pays better to keep friends with white men.

My garrison is rather small at present as 35 men have gone away 12 days march to carry food for Smith, leaving me with about 105 men besides the sick, lame & lazy. Portal also kindly bequeathed me for safe keeping about 130 Nubians, men, women & children, of whom only about 20 are fit for duty on emergency....Some of the Nubians have lost their toes & the greater part of their feet from "jiggers",[14] those beastly insects which are very plentiful in Uganda & I am afraid one or two of the women will die as I can't manage to stop the decaying process. This part of the business is not a nice job but I have got one man who is pretty good for a native at dressing, so I chiefly superintend from a good position to windward....

....From here to Machakos I took my cart drawn by four bullocks & though the last part was a pretty rough passage, brought them in, thus accomplishing the first actual journey made by bullock cart in this part of the world. I capsized twice but did no damage.

Kikuyu. Oct. 3rd 1893

We have had several scares of Masai & one night the Kikuyu people sounded the alarm in every direction so I felt sure they were really coming & got all the Nubian women & children into the Fort & everything ready, sent out pickets &c. but after about 2 hrs. we heard the Kikuyu people returning & it seems that they had seen a few Masai who had run away directly the alarm sounded. However I didn't get much sleep that night & on several nights since I have had to turn out, but have not had to beat to quarters. It is a beastly nuisance for I don't really believe they would ever attempt to attack the Fort but it won't do to be caught napping. Luckily the Kikuyu folk make enough noise to wake the dead when they see any Masai so I have plenty of outlying pickets.

We have sad news from Kismayu where one of our fellows, Hamilton,[15] who was sent up in charge of some of the Sultan's men to keep peace after the last row, has been killed. His own men rebelled, & though he fought gamely to the last, single-handed, was shot through the heart. The men stole all his things & deserted to the Somalis & for days afterwards there were great revels while his body was slowly hacked to pieces....

....I hear there is a Col. Colville[16] coming up with 3 or 4 other officers for Uganda - they will be the next Europeans that I shall see. Luckily my clerk, a Goanese, talks English & is a very decent willing chap so is allowed to come in in the evenings & keep me company. Otherwise I should be at a loss for anyone to talk to, for if I speak to any man in a friendly way he is sure to say that he is very ill, which means he wants to shirk work & thinks you are in such a good humour you won't ask any questions. But some of them fail to come for a second dose of quinine & Calomel mixed; it seems to answer the purpose I concocted it for.

The worst cases I have are the Nubians with their feet nearly gone with jiggers & some cases of dysentery from Smith's caravan, 3 of whom died shortly after Smith had left. I fed one on my own corn flour & milk but, going to see him one day unexpectedly, found him guzzling sweet potatoes & meat & he died two days after. So I am not going to waste any more corn flour.

Kikuyu. Oct. 28th '93

Since my last, the chief event was the arrival here of Col. Colville & party, consisting of Capts. Gibb & Thruston[17] & his caravan leader Mixworthy.... No official intimation had been sent to me from the coast, so they took me by surprise, & as they wanted 50 donkeys, some cattle & sheep & at least 5 tons of food, it was rather a large order to be sprung on one. Colville himself seems very jolly but very eccentric & from all accounts is a bit of a Tartar, but he will soon find that Guards' discipline won't fit with Nubians & as for Europeans, they are much too independent to be bossed round like Tommy Atkins. He told me he had reported all hands at the coast in very strong terms for the way in which he had been treated i.e. with total indifference, but as he also said that he had started with no further instructions than a wire from the Foreign Office "Go to Uganda," no doubt the Mombasa people were in the same plight that I was - no instructions....

....I have reaped the trial crops of wheat & barley & the results are, I think, very fair. One fifth of an acre sown with 36 lbs. of wheat in lines yielded 250 lbs. but a lot had been spoilt by rust before reaping. 2 kinds of barley, each one eighth of an acre yielded 150 lbs. each, all this in new & unmanured ground. For the life of me I can't remember how many lbs. go to a bushel of wheat. Ainsworth can't tell me, so I must discreetly stick to lbs. in my official report. This reminds me I should very much like a "Whitaker's Almanac" for '94. It is an awfully useful thing to have in a place like this & at present there is no such thing as an almanac or diary on the Station, so we have to make our own.

Just at present I am in the thick of a great pow-wow with the Masai. The head Chief of all the Masai sent me a present of two donkeys by two of his headmen with a message to say they wanted to make friends. The Masai about here have always been friendly with white men & are altogether a fine lot. I called a meeting of all the headmen of the Wakikuyu to talk the matter over & it was decided that I would go with 6 of the Wakikuyu headmen & see the Masai Chief & arrange matters. Accordingly last Monday off we went. I took 20 picked men in case of accidents & we had a very jolly walk through the forest by paths for about 3 hrs. when we came on the first camp of the Masai. Here the warriors (Elmoran) turned out & we had to wait while they executed a war dance to a rousing chorus. Then they all stuck their spears in the ground & came up & shook hands. We were then free to pass on to the head kraal, a miserable collection of bush hovels & I took my seat under a shady tree & waited. After a time the Chief came out with the General of Elmoran. I had to seize the Chief's hand & lead him to the cow which I had brought for a present & place his hand on its head. Of course the cow ran away & while they were catching it we stood hand in hand, a fine picture of "brotherly love" & not being able to understand each other we stood there like mutes & I nearly spoilt the solemnity of the game by bursting into laughter. At last 4 men held the brute & then we got a chance of completing the ceremony. After this they wanted me to stop at least one night but luckily, as I had no tent or anything, I got out of it after lots of talk. Then we got to business & for some hours things went swimmingly, but in the middle of it news came in that the Wakikuyu had attacked some Masai & carried off their cattle. This was an awkward contretemps that I had not reckoned on & led to some pretty brisk talk on both sides. However I managed to assure the old chap that we knew nothing of it and that if it was true I would punish the offenders. We were in a bit of a tight corner for there were hundreds of Masai all round & we should have had a tough job to get out if they turned nasty. The onlookers got rather excited & at last the Chief called me on one side & said he always wanted to keep friends with white men but under the circumstances didn't want to have anything to do with the Wakikuyu. This finished the whole thing as of course I couldn't say anything in favour of those blackguards.

Then came a grand war dance by two detachments of Elmoran which was a very fine sight & when they had finished they planted their shields & spears in a semi-circle and all filed up & shook hands. My arm ached for I had shaken hands with at least 500 already & my hand was soon the same colour as theirs.

It was a most funny day altogether. Sometimes, while I was sitting down, one would come up, shake hands & then take off my hat, stroke my hair, pull my beard, pass his hand over my face & then examine my hat, clothes, boots & everything & finish up with a loud "Gai" which means God. My men simply rolled about with laughter though, until I had given the word, my bodyguard were inclined to resent such familiarity. My rifle, revolver, watch, knife, matches & tobacco came in for a share of their curiosity. One would not believe that I could make a real fire, so put his finger over a lighted match but soon shouted "enough" to the delight of the rest. The collection of natives was curious. There were three clans of Masai, some Wakikuyu, while I had my headman, a Baluchi who has been with me since I first came out, 2 Somalis who were Nelson's bodyguard, 10 Nubians &

10 Swahilis.[18] The three first, with my boy carrying my rifle, stuck to me like one shadow the whole day & later the Wakikuyu kept pretty close for they feared vengeance. The Masai behaved very well & are certainly more honourable than most natives. I had arrived at 9 a.m. & at last at 4.15 p.m. I made a start home. The Chief saw us safely past the outlying camp in case of accidents & we got back just before dark. I enjoyed the walk immensely though I was very sick of the continual pow-wow. We afterwards learnt that the news of the fighting was a yarn & the Chief has now sent in to ask me to come again. So I suppose I must repeat the performance as his emissaries have orders to wait & come back with me....

....As to Gregory I'm afraid his trip will do more harm than good by inducing men to go with small escorts. Gregory is a man who will not easily come to grief for the natives look on him as a lunatic & they never harm lunatics. For example, on his return journey he left his men three or four days behind & started over the mountains for Machakos from the N.E. He lost his road & some friendly natives guided him to the Fort. About 9 p.m. one dark night, Ainsworth's sentries came & said there were some natives at the gate who had found a mad white man wandering about & brought him in. A. went out to see, & there was Gregory in rags & very tired. He mildly remarked that his men might turn up in a few days or possibly go by another road to Mombasa. He had travelled in this free & easy way all the time so you may imagine it wasn't his fault....

....I was busy writing this morning, having to start the mail tomorrow morning, when a messenger came in to say the Masai had come halfway to meet the Wakikuyu & they wanted me to come at once. So off I had to go & after a walk of about 3 miles came on large parties of Wakikuyu all armed, & further on a body of Masai squatting in an open plain. I took 20 of my askaris (soldiers) who carry long Snider rifles & sword bayonets & marched up in good form with fixed bayonets. There was the usual pow-wow for about an hour & then, all preliminaries & terms of agreement having been made, were ratified by the slaughter of a goat with great pomp & ceremony. One headman for each party held the goat while my representatives, flourishing the knife, made a great speech. Then the dire effects of breaking such a solemn pledge were enumerated &, from what I could make out, seemed to include all the curses of this world & the next, & for each one a small stick was thrown onto the goat. At last, after another harangue, the head was severed from the body, completing the business. Then arose a mighty shout & both parties executed triumphant war dances, while my Sergeant

Major, not to be outdone, marched my men about in all sorts of formations doing manual & bayonet exercises at lightning speed. The whole scene was extraordinary & very impressive. My men do the bayonet drill very well indeed & fairly astonished Col. Colville & it always impresses the natives. At last all parties mingled & shook hands & pow-wowed all round & then all started for home seeing who could sing the loudest. In this my fellows did well for such a small party....

....By this last mail I got a lot of good things besides some clothes which I had asked Espie to get for me for Xmas. Such a feed I shall have. He sent some whiskey, 2 sherry & actually 2 beer, tinned mince meat, plum puddings (4), stewed fruits, spice, soups, caviar & other delicacies. All these I shall keep for Xmas unless Major Smith turns up before then, in which case we shall probably make an Xmas of our own as one can't enjoy such luxuries alone. The sight of a beer was a sore temptation & had it not been quickly locked away I'm afraid there would only have been one bottle left when Smith came. But now I must shut up as I have to write all my official letters yet & sign & look through about 14,000 returns.

Kikuyu. Nov. 24th '93

I am sorry to say that my Goanese clerk is going to the coast as they have sent another in his place. The poor beggar deserves to get away as he has now been 3 years up-country in the Coy's service, but I shall be sorry to lose him as he thoroughly understands his work & is very willing & useful in many ways. If the new man is half as good I shall be well satisfied. Forty men have arrived, which will allow the oldest hands to get away, & of course there is great jubilee amongst them at the present.

The only event of any importance here was a small shindy with the Wakikuyu, who by virtue of the peace between the tribes, had inveigled some Masai to their kraal & treacherously murdered them in the night. I got the news at 11 p.m. &. knowing they would not expect anything until next day, as they live about 6 miles away, I determined to take them by surprise by prompt action. Luckily several of the friendly Chiefs were with me at the time so I told them to call their men together at once & in less than an hour my men, together with a large party of friendlies, were on the road. The natives had not driven off their stock so my fellows swooped down on them quite unexpectedly & made a grand haul of over 1000 goats & 6 head of cattle. A good deal of ammunition was wasted, chiefly in jubilation, on the way home; however they did kill 9 & wounded 5 with 600 rounds which is above average for Swahili shooting. On our side there were no casualties. This is the severest blow the natives have ever had, as this is the third or 4th occasion that it has been necessary to fight this particular people. I was delighted & felt sure that they would now find out that it pays better to keep friends than to quarrel with white men....

....The next day I counted the spoils; 922 sheep & goats & 6 cattle. Of course a lot of goats had been lost on the road & several were washed away in a river, so the original number must have been well over 1000. The friendlies turned up like vultures, & as the Chiefs said they would share them out, I gave them 350, holding a good reserve for myself & my particular friends. It was well I did so, for after a lot of talk amongst themselves as to shares &c. in which the disputants nearly came to blows, the matter was settled by some young bloods rushing into the flocks & in a moment there was a grand scramble, men, women, children, each catching as many as they could & dragging them off. My men stood apart, cheering & yelling like demons at the fun.

There were some most ludicrous scenes. A little boy hanging on bravely to a goat about twice his size, rolling over & over in the mud & yelling madly to his mother who, quite oblivious of her faithful offspring, was marching off triumphantly, towing two goats by their front legs. In another spot, two boys were struggling madly over one goat which eventually left them to fight it out & was captured by a third party. I felt quite ill with laughing & was half inclined to give them some more to scramble for. But of course the result was that the most deserving got least, but with the balance in hand I was able to make them each a good present & after giving all hands in garrison a good feed (1 goat to 4 men) & sending a cow & 50 goats as recompense to the Masai Chief, I had a balance of 300 to credit of the Station....

....Thank goodness they don't worry me much from the coast. They are too short handed to do more than they can help so we are left to ourselves. I have a grand supply of good things for Xmas, & by this mail the Parsee who worked in the Transport Office under me, sent me a tinned cheese, a camp pie & two plum puddings which were imported by the Mombasa Co-op Stores....

....Since I last wrote I paid a visit to the Masai Chief & slept a night amongst them. I took my tent & bedding as their wigwams are anything but inviting. I had to give them an exhibition of rifle shooting which delighted them. My old hat had to do duty as a target on a tree at 200 yds. & got a few more air holes in it, so it is now well ventilated & would hardly appear respectable out of Kikuyu.

In the morning I held a regular levee of all the bigwigs, but as they insisted on having the pow-wow in my tent with both ends closed, I was not sorry when it was over.

They persisted in saying I was God (Ngai) & amongst others, brought in a little blind girl & a man suffering from fits, to be cured, while the patients suffering from other ailments would have filled my ordinary hospital. Several of the headmen returned with me to the Fort to see its various wonders & a few days afterwards the Chief himself came. For his edification I fired a blue light & a couple of signal rockets which fairly frightened the wits out of them & they all bolted into the huts. When I laughed at them afterwards they chuckled over the fact that lots of my men had bolted as well. They hardly slept at all that night & when I passed to visit the sentries I heard them still describing the rockets in a way that would have delighted certain young ladies of Tonbridge. Their utter ignorance of everything European is perfectly astounding & is often ludicrous. One man looking in a looking glass groped round underneath with his hand to make sure there was really not another in front of him; another put his finger in the flame of a lighted match to see if it was really fire & found it was. One man took too big a sniff of my ammonia & it nearly knocked him down & altogether I had great sport with them.

Amongst their ornaments several wore brass porters' tickets & they also have a Snider Carbine which belonged to the Coy. & sundry other spoils of former raids. Their General, named Legonani told me that in one of their raids they reached the coast near Mombasa, but they didn't wait there as "all the drinking water was so salt." The Elmoran, or warriors, live on meat & sour milk only, but they make up a want of variety by the quantity they consume. A goat of 40 lbs. weight between 4 men for one day is sort of starvation rations. So you may imagine you require plenty of loot to keep them going & a visit from a friendly party of them means an appreciable decrease in the flock. At last I had to ask the Chief to send only 2 or 3 men when he wished to send a message, as parties of 15 or 20 every second day began to get rather beyond my powers of hospitality. He apologized in quite a gentlemanly manner & promised that in future he would send his emissaries in the morning so that they might return the same day, unless I wished them to stay.

Kikuyu. Dec. 14th 1893

I got an awful shock the other day at hearing from Ainsworth that a Missionary[19] with his wife[20] & five children were en route to Kikuyu with the intention of starting a Mission in the District & the shock was considerably intensified by the sudden arrival of the party some days before they were expected. Scott-Elliott turned up one morning as expected & I was delighted to meet him, but imagine my horror when I asked him where the Mission crowd were & he replied "at the tail end of my caravan," & in five minutes I was hustling my boys round to clear my own rooms to accommodate a whole family. Thank goodness I had already had my clothes mended up, so managed to appear passably decent, with my only respectable hat which is kept for State occasions & my coat carefully buttoned up because all the lining is out & I had no buttons on my shirt. In fact, with knickers & stockings I felt rather a swell.

The lunatic is a man named Watt, an Irishman who used to be a traveller in the wholesale tea trade & now a raving lunatic in the Missionary trade. His wife is also Irish & the children are jolly little things ranging from 6 weeks to 6 years old, all as happy & as healthy as can be. They were for some time at Ngongo [Ngong], further South, but nearly got murdered so have come to try these parts. Why they were ever allowed to start from the coast goodness knows. Ainsworth tried all he knew to frighten them out of the place, as did Scott-Elliott & everyone they saw, & when Watt asked me to tell him (the Mrs. was not present) what I honestly thought of his plan, I just rapped out "D----d madness" & Scott-Elliott agreed that it was the only way of expressing it. However he said he wouldn't give it up so I wrote him an official warning of the dangers & told him I would "not be responsible in any way for the lives or property of his party once out of rifle range."....

....Personally they were very nice. They had my two rooms, Scott-Elliott had another. I was relegated to the medicine room & the whole show upside down. However everyone seemed to enjoy themselves & with the good feeding & quarters, seemed more than pleased. They left most of their baggage here & left this morning to go & see Meranga & will probably be back in about 8 or 9 days. I am praying the Wakikuyu will give them a good fright this trip but as they have, together with my men, 50 guns, they can't come to too much harm.

Scott-Elliott is an awful nice chap & I only wish he had been here alone. As it was, I had my hands so full getting all his food, donkeys, saddles &c.

ready, besides having to attend to the Missionaries, that it was only at night after all had gone to roost that we had time to chat, & the three nights he stayed we sat in easy chairs with pipes & a glass of whiskey (sometimes two) & never went to bed before 2 a.m. He is intensely scientific, & has travelled a great deal in all parts of Africa; Egypt, Congo, South Africa, Madagascar &c. & some of his yarns were awfully interesting & I need scarcely say that, as he adapted himself to his company, the conversation was not too scientific. He also left this morning so I feel lonely again.

Notes

1. Sir Gerald Portal, KCMG, Her Majesty's Agent and Consul General in Zanzibar. The IBEA Company's decision to abandon Uganda created uproar in England and nearly brought down Gladstone's Government. Lord Rosebery, British Foreign Secretary, commissioned Portal in December 1892 to proceed to Uganda and report to the Cabinet on the conditions prevailing in that country, with a view to furnishing guidelines for policy. With a party of eight Britons and 600 porters and soldiers he marched the 700 miles from the coast to Kampala in 76 days, arriving on March 17, 1893.

2. Maria Harriette Hall, Francis Hall's sister.

3. Kilimanjaro, 19,340 ft. Highest mountain in Africa.

4. Crocodiles.

5. Later called Ngong, a Maasai town at the foot of the Ngong hills.

6. John Walter Gregory, Professor of Geology and keen explorer. During an extensive safari in East Africa he made an unsuccessful attempt on the summit of Mount Kenya (17,058 ft.) in June 1892, reaching an altitude of 15,580 ft. In his book The Great Rift Valley he painted a pessimistic picture of the region's probable agricultural yield and remarked on its lack of mineral wealth. "I cannot represent British East Africa as a land flowing with milk and honey."

7. Colonel Rhodes DSO, sometime Military Secretary to the Governor of Bombay. Accompanied Portal on his Ugandan mission.

8. Francis Hall's brother Edward Hall.

9. Captain J.H.Williams, artillery officer who reinforced Captain F.D.Lugard in Kampala in January 1891 during the latter's mission to negotiate a treaty with Mwanga, the Kabaka of Uganda.

10. A Bantu people living in the area of Machakos and governed, in Kikuyu fashion, by elders rather than by chiefs. The Wakamba were expert and diligent agriculturists and known for their tracking ability and their lethal arrow poison which was traded as far away as Abyssinia. The German missionary Johann Ludwig Krapf described them in 1848 as "very talkative, noisy, treacherous and greedy," and he noted the custom of filing their teeth to points. They were not hostile to the European invaders and were anxious to make friends.

11. Ernest Gedge, second-in-command to Frederick Jackson on his safari to Lake Victoria in 1889-90. Correspondent of The Times.

12. Sudanese soldiers, described by one official as "having great qualities and serious defects. He has soldier-like instincts, is brave, physically enduring and patient; on the other hand he is, from his very patience, profoundly treacherous." Lugard considered them "the best material for soldiery in Africa."

13. The Arab/Bantu language of the coastal people of East Africa widely used as a lingua franca between tribes. Properly known as Kiswahili.

14. Pulex irritans, a burrowing flea.

15. W.G.Hamilton of the IBEA Company.

16. Colonel the Honourable H.E.Colville, appointed Administrator of the IBEA Company in Uganda, November 1893. Invalided home 1894.

17. Captain A.B. Thruston (later Major). Four years later, in 1897, he commanded the garrison of Sudanese troops at Luba's, Uganda. During the Uganda Mutiny of that year his troops made him and two other Europeans prisoners and handed over the fort to the Sudanese mutineers. The three prisoners were shot. As a result, a force of troops were sent to disarm the Sudanese garrisons of Naivasha and Ravine, an action in which Francis Hall participated.

18. Natives from the coastal region much employed as porters on safaris to Uganda. Captain J.R.L. Macdonald's official survey report for the Uganda Railway described them thus. "On the coast, with a few Rupees in his pocket, the Swahili porter is very often drunk and always lazy. Upcountry he is a very different man. Day after day he will march along under a burning sun, often with very little water to drink; it may be in bad weather, through swamps and swollen rivers, weakened perhaps by fever, with no food but a little sodden flour, and having no better place than the wet, swampy ground on which to rest his head at night, without even a blanket to lie upon, often without a tent to cover him. He is always cheerful, always willing to respond to any call for an extra effort in marching, will remember a kind word for months and forget a punishment directly it is over. His worst points are that he will thieve and get drunk whenever he can conveniently do so." Permanent Way, M.F. Hill, Vol 1 p 71.

19. Rev. Stuart Watt. Pioneer missionary who first visited the Usoga country north of Lake Victoria in 1885, the year of Bishop Hannington's murder. After some years in Australia he returned to East Africa and walked from Mombasa to Fort Smith with his wife and five children.

20. Rachel Watt was the first white woman to travel into the interior of East Africa and stayed for forty three years. She wrote an account of her experiences, In the Heart of Savagedom, Marshall Bros. London 1913.

Map 4 Kikuyu District

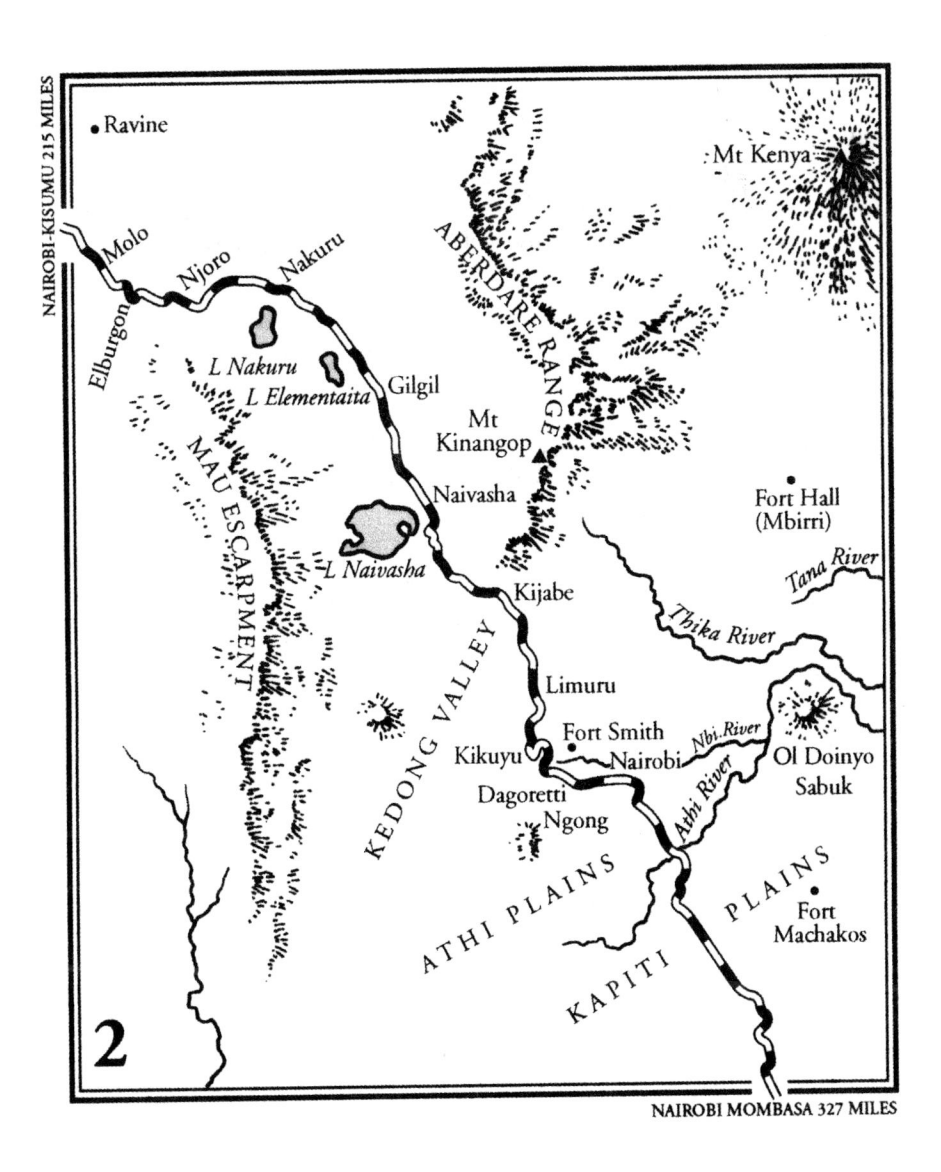

Chapter 3

ENCOUNTERS WITH MISSIONARIES AND RHINOS

Kikuyu. Jany. 14th '94

I think I told you in my last of the awful tidings re the approach of a Missionary with wife & family. They arrived here together with Scott-Elliott & of course I tried all I knew to dissuade them from thinking of staying in the District but they would see for themselves.

They started off to go to a District about 50 miles from here, via Wandengi's. The latter is a friendly old Chief about 15 miles from here & I advised them to sound him out on the subject, sent my own interpreter with them & a present for the old chap. They expected to be away about 10 or 12 days. You may imagine the awful fright I got next night about 9 p.m. when the sentry reported a party approaching & we heard the Swahilis shouting. I rushed out to meet them & found they were alright, but old Wandengi had told them plump he didn't want them there (he was frightened of the responsibility) & also said that the people in the next District, who had just cut up a safari of Swahilis (50 of them), were yearning for more slaughter & would certainly kill the whole party, so they thought it better to return.

One would have thought this would put them off, but no. Watt decided to go round by the Athi Plains & so avoid these particular people. However I persuaded him to leave the wife & children & go by himself with 60 guns. It was much against his grain but I spoke plainly & insisted on his taking plenty of men & ammunition & lent him 10 good men of my own. Of course they advance the good old Missionary song "the Lord would protect them" but I told them that was probably alright in theory but didn't hold good in Kikuyu where the Lord helps those who help themselves. However they took my advice at last & Watt started. I lent him all my own camp gear, as his tents &c. were all his family arrangements weighing tons, & he expected to be back in 10 days. The Mrs. & children made themselves quite at home & were not a bit of trouble & my men wish heartily they would always stop here, for I could never cuss them properly & not a man got flogged while they were here, though some managed to run up a pretty good account which was settled later. However it was very jolly & homely & I rather enjoyed it & all my clothes got mended for once & I buttoned my shirt & sometimes my coat & generally tried to appear respectable, though I did once come in to lunch with my pipe in my mouth & of course was never in time for a meal, but these little details only caused a laugh.

On the 22nd, Major Smith turned up with Martin & Reddie, two former employees of the Coy. & a Missionary from Uganda, so we were a goodly party. They all seemed to feel awkward at first, but Mrs. W. was such a jolly little body they soon shook down. Luckily the Commissariat was fully equal to demands & my little batch of luxuries came in handy.

Watt returned unexpectedly, having been stopped by full rivers & I was very glad of it as he was able to get the Major's opinion on his plans which was curt, emphatic & anything but scripturally expressed.

On Xmas Day we all decided to shave off our beards to celebrate the occasion & consequently hardly knew each other at breakfast. The Major & I were hard at work all day preparing for the departure of his caravan of 550 men. We had to get nearly 5000 lbs. of food served out & he handed over all his surplus guns &c. for safe keeping pending his return in April.

The Major's cook, a Mission native, undertook the dinner & I gave out all the things & left him to it. The children had theirs at mid-day & as I had a tin of mixed biscuits, plum pudding & preserved ginger, jam & honey galore, they had a regular jubilee & were as happy as mudlarks.

The Major & I thanked God devoutly that all the others refused beer at lunch. There were only two bottles so we had one each & a grand treat it was. Martin was the only one who made us unhappy, as he hesitated over the beer. But the Major promptly assured him that for a man with a liver it was certain death, so he took sherry.

The dinner was quite a success; ox-tail soup, fricatelles, roast fowl, roast saddle of mutton, plum pudding, sweet omelet & sundry other minor dishes. The great fun was the cook who didn't understand what the mincemeat was, though he made a grand great mince pie, and it was served up as an entree trimmed with parsley & it was only on tasting it we found out for certain what it was. Then, once tasted, it was too good to wait for, so we ate it all & then continued dinner without further troubles. For afternoon tea Mrs. Watt made some tea cakes of which we all ate far too many & altogether we had a very jolly day. In fact I expect I shall spend many a worse Xmas in Africa. Taking the whole circumstances of place &c., nothing could have been jollier & long chairs & pipes round the fire after dinner finished the day nicely.

Watt had decided on returning to Machakos, & as the Major offered to carry any surplus loads, he took the chance & they all left on the 26th.[1] Of course I felt terribly lonely & what with worries about some of the Wakikuyu &c. fairly got a fit of the jim-jams.

I had sent some men out to buy food on Xmas Day & they returned empty handed having been warned by some friendly natives that a trap had been laid for them & unless they cleared off at once they would all be murdered. I sent a messenger to enquire into the matter but he was caught & beaten, all his arms & ornaments taken away & he had to run for his life. I then sent three friendly Wakikuyu to gather news but they ran back as soon as they saw danger....I started my men off at 1 in the morning & they reached the place 6 miles off in good time & surrounded the kraals & at daybreak got to business....My fellows fought splendidly I hear & as the enemy came so close, couldn't miss them & the slaughter was heavy, but at last the natives got sick of it & drew off. As usual some of my men lost their heads & the Sergt. Major with only five men rushed to cut off some cattle, with the result that they were at once surrounded, 2 killed & 3 wounded, & but for timely assistance all would have perished. These were the only casualties on my side & I have since heard the enemy lost over 90 killed, of which the Chief was one of the first. My men were all shot with poisoned arrows, but luckily I gave the clerk some ammonia & whiskey to take with them & told him how to use it & this no doubt saved their lives....

....The Sergt. Major got the only nasty wound through the inside of the upper arm, just missing the artery, & the fool of a Goan never took the arrow head out. Directly they got here I attended to him, though I was afraid it was too late for he was already quite drowsy. But I poured whiskey & ammonium into him & poulticed the wound every quarter of an hour & though he was slightly delirious in the night, he got better as the poison returned to his arm which swelled out like a football, & after a few days continual poulticing he was practically alright though he is not yet on duty....I'm very pleased about the Sergt. Major's recovery as it has given the men confidence. Formerly they reckoned a scratch from a poisoned arrow meant death, & I must say I never relished the idea of getting one, but I know what to do for them now....

....My new Goanese clerk was very anxious to go and see the fun, so I put him under the wing of my headman. The march alone half killed him & he certainly got more frighting than he either expected or cared for, though he did his share bravely & never flinched. His boy was floored by a knobkerrie by his side & he promptly shot the assailant. In fact he did very well but he doesn't hanker after any more trips of that kind.

Lots of the men were badly bruised by knobkerries thrown by natives but as nothing less than a steam hammer would have any permanent effect on their skulls they were all on parade next day. Though very sorry to lose two men needlessly, I am very pleased at the conduct of my men & after the lecture last time, they were very careful of the ammunition & averaged only 9 rounds per man which is very good for 90 killed & I'm sure beats all previous Swahili records.

A few days later they sent a witch-doctor to make medicine near here, so that I & all the friendly natives should die, but some friendly natives caught & killed him promptly, so the chances are against his medicine having any effect. They have now sent word for another doctor, but my fellows are on the lookout & the supply of doctors will be likely to run short before long if they are not careful.

This business has been a bit of a worry & then my clerk has made an awful mess of the a/cs & for the life of me, though I have tried for days & nights, I can't pan them out. The system is so complicated & there are so many forms & returns to be filled, that no one who has ever seen a/cs before can understand them, & as this is the clerk's first month I can't blame him....

....The present unsettled state of the Coy. is very unsatisfactory but I hope we shall soon know what is going to happen. Our staff out here is rapidly decreasing; there are now only 7 Europeans in Mombasa, some 3 or 4 at other Coast Stations & Ainsworth & I up-country. In fact, generally, the show seems to have gone to the dogs.

Pigott, the Actg. Adminstr. has married a Missionary & I hear from the other fellows that prayer meetings are the chief feature of the day's proceedings. Not that any of the others attend them, but their absence causes a sort of tension, & as the Missionaries rule the roost it is none too pleasant....

....The C.M.S. does not allow ladies up-country, they are all quartered at Mombasa or at Frere Town down the harbour. They have splendid quarters, live well & their occupation consists of praying, psalm singing in the streets, lawn-tennis, boating, drawing pay & having periodical trips to England, while some of the more fortunate ones manage to hook an Administrator or a Vice-Consul, a far more important object than converting our black brethren.

When people like Watt, who came out at his own expense & on his own hook, appear on the scene, the C.M.S. people stand aloof & treat him as a pariah. He actually had to pitch his tent near Mombasa. Not one of these Christians would offer him a roof for a few days. If Eusty[2] can't get anything else I should advise him to study the Bible for a month & then apply to the C.M.S. They will (if he talks Bible properly) not only give him £100 a year & good quarters &c., but if he likes to get married they will provide for his wife & everything. It is one of the softest jobs I know of. They prefer grocers' or drapers' clerks who have taught in a Sunday school, but perhaps they might not object to a gentleman for a change, & if he volunteered to evangelise the Kikuyu, they would promise him double pay because they know he wouldn't live to draw it. We love Missionaries in Africa. I wonder how some of the poor old ladies who give their spare coin would like to see the show in Mombasa & hear the Missionaries chuckling over the fact that the revenue of the Society is over a quarter of a million. The whole thing is sickening & should be exposed....

....Smith brought a grand collection of ivory from Uganda. The biggest tusk was 194 lbs. & was bought by MacDonald & the Major as a wedding present for the Duke of York. It is a magnificent piece, 8 ft. long & very thick. Fancy any animal carrying the pair of these. The mate was only 191 lbs. Each of these was carried by two porters from Uganda to Mombasa & they consider it a great honour to be picked out for such a job. For myself, I should prefer to do without such honours....

....I have only just succeeded in finishing the last of the a/cs. Never no more do I bother my head like this for the Coy. or anyone else. If the clerk can't get them right they may stay wrong for all I care. And now to bed.

Kikuyu. Feby. 12th '94

Your letters of 1st & 9th December reached yesterday & the posting of the Graphics was so successful that the latest date is 21st. of Dec. & as these reached here on 10th. it puts me only 51 days behind the news of the world which is not bad considering all things....

....It seems that Lenana[3] & his Masai got into sad straits for food &c. & were being considerably harassed by the Kilimanjaro Masai & driven from pillar to post. At last, one night, about 15 of them came in here & said their women & children (about 30) were out in the bush & wanted to come & live under my protection. I discussed the matter with a friendly Chief who is my fidus Achates & as we knew they would be captured as slaves if we didn't protect them, I sent off a party of men to escort them in. Of course I knew the Masai were lying when they said about 30 people & I expected about 100, but when they began to arrive about 4 p.m. & my escort behind was not in sight, I was thunderstruck. The Kikuyu Chief turned up roaring with laughter & when I asked him how many there were, said he didn't know but "if I were to give out all my goats (about 350) they would not go round."....

....There was nothing for it but to do the best we could, so I first of all pointed out a spot to build between Kinanjui's village & the Fort, & K. has given them a lot of land close handy to cultivate. I called the Legonan (Chief) & told him it was impossible for me to feed such a crowd but he said they would look after themselves. All they wanted was protection & they would do anything I ordered....

....In spite of previous warnings & examples, another attempt was made on the cattle kraal. I had warned all the sentries if they saw a thief about, to let him get close before challenging, & if he ran, to shoot low & straight. I was writing my diary when "bang" from the Nubian Post. I rushed out & found the sentry had obeyed my instructions. He challenged sharp & the man turned & ran but got the bullet right through the back & lungs & was dead when I got there....

....Two nights ago the same thing happened but had an even more tragic ending. The Nubians fired a shot & on enquiry they said three men had come close up but had run at the first challenge & got away. I started as usual to search round with the Nubians & my orderly, to try if we could find or hear something. After some time I decided to give it up & get back to bed & was returning when I saw a black object which didn't seem to be part of the stump it was close against. Stooping low with the revolver covering it, I challenged several times but no move or answer. I then said to the men "what is it?" & stepped up to kick it when it rose & before I could speak, the Nubians emptied their rifles into him & he rolled over....

....The Masai Legonan was most philosophic over it. He said, "whether he came to steal or not, God sent him there to die & he died."

They have funny ideas of a Supreme Being (Ngai). Everything they don't understand is Ngai. They say all white men are Ngai. Anything they see, such as a clock; I have one alarm clock which always fetches them, or a looking glass or such like is Ngai & requires no further comment. Of course being the only white man with whom they have been in such close contact I am Ngai. Altogether I like them immensely. They are happy, free & easy people with few cares & up to date have given me no trouble & obeyed all orders implicitly.

Their salutations are somewhat embarrassing as each man hugs you round the waist with his right arm & puts his face close to yours as if to kiss you. This operation performed by nearly 100 of them returning from a fight on a hot day is not pleasant. The women shake hands, and as the time when I see most of them is in the morning when they are collecting the cow-dung out of the kraal to plaster their huts, the performance is also somewhat trying. After the first morning I was careful & refused resolutely, but I still get caught unawares occasionally. When they first meet you they also spit on you for luck & they always spit at cattle & goats. I have been spat on so often that I have got quite used to it now....

....My new clerk is not exactly a success, either as a clerk or companion. His conversational powers are not only limited but also distinctly aggravating. For instance yesterday, after I had read my letters, he asked if there was any news.

"Nothing much," said I, Bruce one of the Directors is dead."

HE: (vacantly) "One of the Directors - what?"

I: "Dead!!!"

HE: "One of the Directors dead - who?"

I: "Bruce!!! One - of - the - Directors - is - dead."

HE: "Oh!!! Oh!!! Oh yes, my friend mentions that in his letter."

Now what is one to do with a man like that for a companion? The only man you see from month to month who can speak English, at least if you call it speaking English. This is not an exceptional conversation (except for length) but an illustration of his regular habit. The last chap, from lengthy companionship with Europeans up-country had some savvy & was a good companion, but this chap fairly beats me hollow, so I keep more to myself than before.

I expect MacDonald here very shortly with probably one or two more Uganda men. I was in a bit of a flutter for there was drought in the land, the whiskey was all done & I know how they look forward to good things on arrival here, but my guardian angel at Mombasa, Espie, had remembered my standing order, "when in doubt send whiskey & tobacco" & to my delight the mail men brought a box containing six bots. of whiskey & some tobacco for which I am only charged cost price, no carriage & a present of a box of cigars. As I still have two hams, 2 Dutch cheeses, several home-made cheeses & lots of tinned stuff, I shall be able to keep up the old Kikuyu traditions.

The garden has suffered a bit from drought, though I have all hands watering occasionally, but there are plenty of tomatoes, lettuces, French beans, green peas, vegetable marrows & onions, so we can get along. I have just dug one bed of potatoes (7 yds. x 48 yds.) about 600 lbs. weight & have another bed ready to dig nearly the same size. The wheat & barley have lasted well and we have good bread every day, so one might have worse living. Duck or goose, green peas & new potatoes has been the standing order for the last 10 days & today the Nubians have presented me with the best part of a leg of beef which is a great treat. It seems it is the Arab feast just now which they keep & they brought me the most wonderful collection of dough-boys, fat cookies, meat and other indescribable dishes that I have yet seen in Africa. In a fit of mental aberration I had promised to eat of their feast & this was the result. However thank goodness they did not wait to see me operate, & all I know is if the boys are as sick tomorrow as the dog was today, I shall not regret having distributed these greasy compounds....

....My latest pet here is a baboon. He belonged to one of the men & has been on the Station for a year or more. He & my dog "Romp" are such great chums that I persuaded the chap to let me have him for 12 yds. of calico.

I made an experiment at keeping small birds & got a splendid assortment but such a lot died that I gave it up & let the rest go. Romp has turned out a grand dog though hardly equal to his father "Shetani," but he is a jolly companion & very faithful to me in spite of being petted and spoilt by my boys. He is quite one of the garrison & always goes round with me to inspect the guards of a night & generally manages to have a run after an hyaena as an opiate before returning to my room.

Kikuyu. March 15th '94

I have just heard from Major Smith that a Major Cunningham is coming up & will be here in a few days to wait here for Smith's arrival some time after. So I shall have company for a few days anyway & as he brings 200 men, which will ensure the safety of the Fort, I may induce him to come out for a few days shooting....
....You might well be surprised at how we get goods up here, especially luxuries, as the usual cost is 33/- a load carriage, but these things are made up in small loads of 25 lbs. each & carried by the mail men, a privilege we are allowed occasionally gratis, & as I do not want to trouble them too often, they do not complain when I send rather a large order. For instance my Xmas order was 6 small loads & without my saying a word about it, they sent me word that I should not be charged. In all these little arrangements the coast fellows are awfully good & I am well looked after by my chums....
....The news of Sir Gerald Portal's death is a sad blow for East Africa & may make a deal of difference to some of us personally. I must find out Col. Rhodes' address & worry him for the photos for I should like to have some memento of our last meeting here. The group consisted of Sir Gerald, Col. Rhodes, Major Smith, Martin, Purkiss & myself & will make a good souvenir of some of the best known men in these parts; Smith, Martin & Purkiss all being old hands & great friends of mine....
....Our rainy season commenced on 1st. with a grand overture by the full band; 2.96" fell within 12 hours. However this seems to have exhausted the supply pro-tem for though it has been very cloudy, we have not had very much since. I have built a stone magazine in one bastion of the Fort, stone roof & all, & got all explosives into it, so I feel more comfortable than I otherwise should with so much lightning about. The old ammunition store had a clay ceiling under the thatched roof which would probably have been some protection against fire, but war-rockets, signal-rockets & about 25,000 rounds of ball cartridge are not pleasant things to have under a thatched roof at any time, & as there are also about 30,000 percussion caps & a few tins of gunpowder, they would make a bit of a mess of the Fort if they did go bust....
....I am getting together a bit of a menagerie here by way of diversion. Up to

date it consists of 2 parrots, a monkey, a dog & a Thomsonii, a lovely little antelope which I have fostered on to a goat & is thriving. He sleeps in the dining room with the dogs & is perfectly happy. My tame partridges have disappeared, probably into a Swahili's soup, but this I can't find out.

My Nubian sentries shot another man the other night with a most extraordinary shot. It passed through behind the knee from side to side of one leg only, not touching the bone but severing the artery & though he was still alive when I found him & I stopped the bleeding at once, he had already lost so much blood that he never rallied. I felt sorry for the poor beggar being killed by such an awful fluke shot, but if they will come fooling round here at night & not answering the challenge, I can't help it....

....I have had a case of meteorological instruments sent up; enough to fit out any ordinary observatory & all to be observed 4 times a day. However the mercury in the barometer absolutely refuses to descend at all, so one observation of that is quite sufficient. The other thermometers, radiometers, solar radiation thermometers & all sorts of other ometers are still in the coffin they arrived in, awaiting the arrival of the Astronomer Royal or some such competent person before I mess about with them. They are apparently much too delicate & valuable for any amateur to fool around with. I thought I could manage the barometer & have already 4 thermometers & a rain gauge here, quite enough for me for the present. If they want any further observations they must send an expert to make them. I can't. The most valuable part to me is the huge deal coffin which would make a lovely store cupboard but I suppose I mustn't break it up.

Kikuyu. April 15th '94.

There is a wonderful change in the Wakikuyu since I first came here. Fancy, the other day I got a deputation to ask if I would hold a meeting with the Chiefs to talk over matters. Of course I agreed, & about 70 Chiefs representing most of the people within a radius of 15 miles came in. It was a long tedious pow-wow but at least they all agreed to acknowledge my authority & to refer all disputes & other matters to me & generally to work in unison, & that if any party offended or caused fighting, they would all assist to wipe them out. Altogether it was a most satisfactory meeting, & as they had planned it entirely amongst themselves & evidently settled all points before bringing them before me, it shows a considerable advance in the right direction. Of course I don't trust them any more than before, but am very pleased to think they have even got so far as to condescend to discuss affairs, instead of fighting first & discussing afterwards.

Kikuyu. May 12th '94

    Captain MacDonald is at last fairly started for home. He arrived here the other day, & after a couple of days rest went on, as he wished to arrange some urgent matters at Zanzibar & get away by French Mail 4th. June. He looks terribly aged after his trying time in Uganda, but is awfully enthusiastic on the general outlook & has considerably raised my spirits as to future prospects. Of course he is the best authority there is now, for he not only surveyed the Railway route but was Portal's Chief Adviser in Uganda, & when Portal had mapped out his scheme roughly, MacDonald was requisitioned to work out all details, so thoroughly understands the whole thing. He says he finds now that they can work considerably cheaper than originally estimated & hopes to get the ear of the powers that be when he arrives home....

....He asked me officially if I was willing to stay here in command if the Govt. took over the Station & the Directors sanctioned transfer. Of course we talked over such important details as leave & free passage home &c. and you may safely say I agreed to his terms which of course are subject to sanction, & on my part to the Directors agreeing to cancel my agreement. The terms are £250 a year & £50 a year for my Swahili. Service of 2 years with Coy. to count so that after 1 yr. I shall be entitled to six months leave on full pay & free passages. I think this is good enough for a start, especially when I can still stay here & save most of my pay....

....The road from here to Mombasa is practically good now for wagons & once started we shall soon see things move. MacDonald was delighted with my turn out, & though he wouldn't ride himself, preferring to march the whole road, I took some of his sickly men on the cart to the outside of the forest to show what could be done & he was awfully pleased both with the cart & the road, I walked to the Nairobi [River] with him as I did in Nov. '92 & we parted at the same spot....

....They do send the most extraordinary officers to Uganda that they can find, as far as health goes. Colville has only one lung left; Gibb has hardly left his quarters since he reached there because of rheumatism; Thruston is subject to epilepsy & Cunningham is physically weak & does not look like lasting long. The Doctor who has gone up to allow Moffat[1] to get away on leave for 12 months cannot march a mile. He gets on a donkey when leaving camp

& never dismounts until he reaches the next camp, unless the donkey falls in a hole or donga & then, the Major says, he always remounts & makes the donkey carry him out of the hole he pitched him into. He was in ecstasies to find my cart awaiting them at the Athi River, 2 days march from here, & promptly got in & slept the whole march. This was alright across the plains, but coming through the forest next day, the wild pigs made straight for it & capsized the cart suddenly & the Doctor woke up in a thorn bush. Martin, who was close behind, shrieked with laughter & the porters who don't care for old womanish white men joined in. The Doctor got no pity & at last had to join in the laughter himself. He is an awful old woman, but a gentleman, which is a great thing....

....I have had a long spell of Africa & on the whole have kept my health better than most men, especially considering the knocking around & rough times I have had. I feel quite equal to another 14 years of it if I am spared so long. The life suits me & if I can get my leave every 3 years I shall be better off than most fellows in India. I have a good climate & feeding, plenty of sport at times, a jolly life comparatively & can't spend my pay here if I try, unless I do as Colville does & have claret & champagne up by mail runners, which costs him 120 Rupees a load, carriage 50 lbs.

Kikuyu. June 10th. '94

The news that Govt. has voted £50,000 for Uganda is decidedly good & a resume of Portal's report, together with what I gleaned from MacDonald & other sources, convinces me that we shall have the Railway as far as here & the country properly opened up, which will be a good thing.

I wonder whether my memo on Kikuyu has been published by now. If so I hope to see it & any remarks that are made on it. They are very fond of publishing Ainsworth's & as they have never had anything of the kind on this District, it will be the more appreciated....

....The news of Uncle John's recovery was indeed good - it takes a lot to knock over one of the Hall family as I have found out more than once, & if only livers had been forgotten in our internal organisation we should be still better. I had been worried a good deal with liverish attacks from want of exercise so I started off the other day, marched to the Athi, 24 miles, did two days tramping about shooting & then back. Though I felt a bit stiff afterwards it did me more good than all the medicine in my dispensary. You can imagine how vastly things have improved here with the natives when I actually risked 4 days absence from the Fort & nothing happened of any moment during that time....

....I had a terrible loss the other day. My best cart bullock died from spanziegte, over-eating on too rich grass. They never told me he was sick until he rolled over dead & then I rushed off to the cattle, dissected him & found out the cause and was luckily in time to save three others by bleeding profusely. I now hear that lung sickness has broken out some distance from here....I have sent out strict orders that no cattle are to travel about the District & none to be brought into the District from Machakos, where Ainsworth warned me it had broken out some fortnight ago.

With regard to this I had a most amusing message today. An Mkikuyu turned up just when I was conferring with my fidus Achates "Kinanjui," the Kikuyu Chief who lives just alongside & has always been loyal to the Europeans, & said he brought news. On enquiry he told me he brought a message from a great mganga (medicine man) of the Wakikuyu. This mganga, during the storm of Tuesday 5th went up on a peal of thunder to God & stayed with him two nights & then returned. God told him that a great plague would shortly visit the District & kill lots of people & also that no cattle must enter the District from Ukambani[5] (Machakos) or all our cattle would die. To be spared from this plague, Kinanjui was to kill a sheep, cut off its head & bury the head underground near the stream to the East, then eat the meat. I was to do likewise, burying the head near the stream to the West. The plague would pass us by & go on to Machakos. Kinanjui, on hearing it, said it must be true for I had already told them about the cattle, though he couldn't quite make out how I had got ahead of the mganga's authority without the aid of thunder. But he begged me to allow him to perform the ceremony, & as it is just as well to humour their little fads, I said alright, but stipulated the head was not to be buried too near the water. It was somewhat difficult to keep my countenance throughout the recital & I couldn't help telling Kinanjui I thought the mganga was a fool to return once he got up there, but he assured me solemnly that this mganga often went, & his father before him the same, so I thought it better not to laugh at their little superstition which, after all, is no worse than many superstitious ideas still held by some educated people at home....

....I received a visit from some of the Wakikuyu from Meranga, the District at the foot of Kenia. They are a far more peaceful lot than those about here & begged me to come up there & establish a Station just now. I gave them a letter & a flag in case the Freelanders[6] should want to come there & promised to visit them the first chance I get. I hope next mail to be able to tell you I am in Govt. service for I hope they will arrange for this Station as soon as possible.

Kikuyu. July 5th '94

By this mail I received most astonishing news. The Coy. has definitely decided to retain all this part of the country. They have taken a contract to carry 120 loads a month from here to the Ravine, 12 days march, the Uganda Admtr. receiving the loads there. For this purpose 200 more men are being sent up here & a European, a Mr. T. M. de Winton, as my assistant; & last but not least, my pay is to be raised to Rs 360 per month. With their usual forethought they send me this news with orders to build extra store-houses and barracks about a month before the men will arrive. In addition to this I am getting a lot of caravans just now & food is terribly scarce, so that I don't know where to turn or what to do and to crown all, these beastly locusts come over in swarms just as I have got all hands to work & I have to pack every soul into the fields to save my crops....

....This is to be the depot for Uganda & I have to store regularly 300 loads as part of the contract. Already I have received 100 to be ready for Smith & 250 more will arrive on the 8th or 9th, & I expect de Winton about the end of the month, the contract commencing on 15th Sept.

What my clerk will do with all these caravan a/cs I don't know. He loses his head completely over the stock-taking & a/c business so will probably commit suicide after two months of this extra work. I am glad to say my old headman, who has been with me ever since I came out, has returned from leave & has also brought back several of my old hands amongst the relief party. It helps me a great deal knowing that I have a few men that I can depend on for work without standing over them with a sjambok.[7] It was awfully good of this man "Abdul"; he remembered that my watch had struck work long ago so he brought a watch for me as a present. It is of course only a common one, but goes well, & for all purposes is as good as the best....

....When I last wrote I think I mentioned there was a bit of a Donnybrook on between the Masai & the Wakikuyu. That night I got 2 & a quarter hours sleep & at daylight the war-cry sounded all around the country. The hills were soon black with Wakikuyu & things began to look a bit serious for the Masai, for I was afraid I should not be able to hold the Fort against such numbers. I sent for some of the Chiefs & told them that any man who approached too close would be fired on, so they went off & told the people & then came back & we had a great pow-wow. I tried a man for killing a Mkikuyu, having 2 Wakikuyu & 2 Masai to form a board, & after hearing all the evidence found him guilty, gave him 100 lashes at once before all hands

& then put him in chains to go to the coast. This pacified the Wakikuyu a bit, but they begged me to send some of the Masai out of the country as there were too many. In this I quite agreed; in fact I had warned the Masai about it myself....

....The following day I started the Masai off with an escort of 40 men. These Kikuyu followed them out of the bush &, after my men had returned, fell on the Masai & carried off as many women & children as they could & killed many more. You may reckon I was a bit mad when I heard of it. I called the Chiefs at once & after cursing them until language failed me I ordered them to return all the Masai they had captured & pay a fine of 100 goats within 3 days or I would wipe them off the face of the earth....

Kikuyu. Aug. 6th '94

Our mails are improving considerably thanks to Ainsworth's natives who run it down very sharp. Fancy, my last mail reached Mombasa in 12 days, pretty good going on foot for 350 miles....

....I have been digging into my old friends in the hills again & have made things lively. Some of the brutes murdered two of our men within half a mile of the Fort. I was on their trail pretty sharp with 20 guns & a yelling horde of Masai, but the whole thing was evidently premeditated, for I found they had already cleared out of the bush with their livestock. I was fairly mad for I had seen one of my old hands, the man who dressed the lion skins & had been with me for a long time, hacked to pieces & I thirsted for revenge.... We made a mess of all their villages & as the other column was working along about 2 miles off, the natives had a warm time of it; but they wouldn't stand so I had no chance of trying my war-rockets. The Major, with his one arm, carried a shot gun & bagged a brace in the first kraal, but I had no fun for a long time & being deadly tired, was somewhat disappointed, for we hoped they would stand & we should have a big fight & smash them once for all....We reached the Fort at 5 p.m., as the Major said "done to a turn." I never experienced such an awful time. We had marched from 8.15 p.m. until 11.30 a.m. without resting & then from 1 p.m. to 5 over the most awful country it is possible to conceive....This has had a marvellous effect on the natives as they thought we couldn't reach them out there, but they still come & lie up in the scrub to kill any man who strays....I called up all the friendly Chiefs & told them that in future any man seen carrying a spear or shield near the Fort would be shot first & interrogated later. They have obeyed alright & only carry sticks, so there is likely to be less bloodshed now. I also told them that unless they took to work like other natives, they would eventually be wiped out & better people brought into the country & the general effect has been wonderful. I got 30 of them to carry food loads for Smith for two or three days & when I called for 100 to go to Machakos to fetch loads for me, over 170 turned up & 105 were written on & brought the loads in good time & were delighted with their pay....This is the first time the Wakikuyu have ever carried loads, so it is a feather in my cap. How long the fit will last remains to be seen but I hope, by letting them down a bit easy at first, that they will get into the way of it. On 1st Aug. my new Asst. turned up with part of the new draft. He is a "de Winton," cousin of Sir Francis, the Duke of York's right hand man & his people used to live at Dulverton. He is a very good sort as far as I have seen & I think we shall fit pretty well. He is a year older than I am & has spent all his time in India but came to smash over coffee planting in the Wynaad & has since been kicking around Burmah. His Indian ideas will have to be worked out of him for they won't fit Swahilis, but I hope he will get along alright for he appears a bit down on his luck....

....My predecessor here, Purkiss, came down from Uganda the other day. He has been very ill up there with haematuric fever & is invalided home on leave. He says he would rather be in Kikuyu on 300 tin tokens a month than in Uganda on £500 a year, for the sovereigns are not much good when a man can only digest Liebig & cornflour. He was a bit of a wreck when he reached here but I made him stay a week & he pulled up wonderfully. De Winton doesn't look strong & says he can't stand cold, so I am not sure he will stand this climate.

Kikuyu. Sept. 3rd '94

Poor old Purkiss; in spite of his stay here which picked him up wonderfully, he developed his haematuric fever again on the road & died at Kibwezi. This was a terrible blow to all of us for he looked so fit when we last saw him. The little Doctor Charters wrote me a very nice letter about it. He did all he knew for Purkiss but it was too late, for he died 30 hrs. after he was carried in. We half-masted the flag here for him, poor old chap. Nelson, he & I were here together in Nov. '92 & I am the sole survivor now. Quick work but one gets accustomed to it in Africa....

....We are just having a good shower of cold rain which I hope will finish off the locusts. In spite of all my trouble they have damaged my wheat & barley very considerably & the continual tramping of men up & down the rows has so hardened the ground that the crop has not had much chance of growing decently. However I hope to harvest enough to keep me in bread for the next year & shall hope to do better next season.

I have actually received orders to forward any surplus stock of potatoes to Mombasa by every available opportunity, as the supply there is so uncertain by ships from Bombay. Fancy sending potatoes 350 miles by porters! But I believe it will pay so shall try a load or two & a load of chilis....

....I expect to hear very shortly that the Govt. has taken over the Administration & then it remains to be seen what they will do with me. I certainly hope for Govt. service as they pay in Sterling, no "tin tokens." De Winton, after my six days absence, was heartily sick of it & fails to understand how I have stood it all this time. He'll get a 20 days spell of it now which will probably finish him off. While he was alone an Mkikuyu was caught lurking in the bush, armed, & was brought in. De W. disarmed him & let him go but he had hardly got out of the gate when he seized a spear & ran amok among the men. He was buried that afternoon, in fact very little was left of him, I believe, by the time de W. arrived on the scene. My men do love these people.

Kikuyu. Oct. 22nd '94

Well here I am, back again for another spell of imprisonment after my holidays. Of course I have had a very bad liver attack since my return, but very slight fever with it, & though still compelled to restrain my voracious appetite, I think I am pretty fairly over it.

The Govt. officer who was to have gone up with me to receive my loads at the Ravine never arrived in time, nor did he write to say where he was. I stuck to my contract time & he came loafing along two days later. Perhaps it was just as well, for our styles of marching were very different. I do the usual thing; get off at 5 in the morning & reach the next camp at latest by 11 a.m., thus avoiding the intense heat at midday & the regulation thunderstorm about 2 or 3 p.m. He never started before 8 a.m. & was simply killing his men. My safari consisted of 140 men & 34 donkeys carrying food, just a nice little caravan. My first day was a very heavy one to the top of mountains, 18 miles, & as two of the donkeys proved utterly useless as travellers, I was marching from 7 a.m. to 5 p.m. & felt terribly done.

The view from this camp is certainly one of the grandest in Africa, it is so vast. You look over an immense deep valley some 30 miles broad & on all sides are gigantic volcanoes towering into the air. It is on such an immense scale that one fails to take it all in. The descent from here is pretty sharp & sudden, as may be imagined from the Railway Survey which measures the drop as 1700 ft. in three miles....Two days march from here has brought us to the shores of Lake Naivasha. A river running into the Lake from the North was impassable so I had to go right round the lake, an extra day's march, but the scenery more than repaid the extra trouble. The lake is a magnificent sight, about 15 miles long by 9 broad & surrounded by volcanic hills with a range of mountains in the background, a most perfect picture....

....Next day we marched round the south end of the lake, a lovely walk, close to the water's edge the whole way. We pitched camp on the side of a hill opposite a vast bed of reeds which was simply alive with waterfowl. I bagged a dozen flamingos with 3 charges of shot, for the men, & a brace of ducks with a fourth for myself so you can imagine they were pretty thick. I afterwards shot 3 flamingos with one bullet. The men like these immensely; they are so beautifully fat, though tough & rank in flavour. The mosquitoes were something too awful in camp & were nearly as big as the flamingos.

The next day we had, for me, a new experience. We were marching down a narrow gorge with high rocks on both sides. I was in the rear when I suddenly saw men & loads flying in all directions. Thinking they must have disturbed an old rhino, I rushed up most gallantly. I had hardly the time to ask what was the matter when a bee stung me in the eye. Business was soon much too brisk for one hand so I put down my gun. Meanwhile they swarmed under the brim of my hat, round my neck, in my eyes & every exposed part & I was soon off at my best pace, shedding pipe & rifle at various stages of my mad career. You couldn't see the dog for dust; poor brute, he had fits at first, for he insisted on sitting down to bite them out, until he found there was more work than one dog could do, then he went. When I had safely ensconced myself on a rock in full view, though a very safe distance from the battlefield, saw heads peeping from under bushes & boulders, some men stretched out like corpses covered with their blankets & loads scattered all over the place. After about half an hour I returned cautiously & recovered my lost property, but while putting a load on my man's head, was stung again in my right eye, & as I already had a head like a pumpkin, I left the rest of the job to the men & beat a hasty retreat with the excuse that I would go back & find another road for the donkeys. I can stand most things, but a flight of good old African rock bees would rout the best army in the world. I was very lucky not to lose any men, for the Railway Survey had two men stung to death under similar circumstances. Our camp that night was again on the main road N.W. of Naivasha. The second river which here runs into Naivasha was brimming full, so my extra day's march had not been in vain. From here we reached a camp on the side of a hill above Lake Elmentaita, a salt lake, much smaller than Naivasha but very pretty. Big game had been scarce but I shot a couple of zebra for the men & a great prize in the shape of the Great African Bustard (Otis kori),[8] very rare, a gigantic bird standing about 3ft. 6in. high & weighing about 150 lbs. & beautiful eating. A leg alone would hardly go into the pot so I had to cut steaks off him. The cold in these parts at night is something deadly & I found four blankets none too warm. The next march, along the hills above the lake, was very pretty & I got some shooting, bagging a zebra, Granti & Thomsonii. This is the best bit of the country for farming or ranching, plenty of water with a good fall, beautiful grass & timber close handy. It used to be swarming with Masai & they certainly were good judges of cattle country. We had to negotiate two bad swamps and then crossed some open plains. I never saw anything like the herds of zebra on these plains, they beat even the Athi, & so tame that they stood at less than 100 yds. & stared at us, but as I couldn't carry the meat, I didn't fire a shot. Nearing the camp on Lake Nakuru I caught sight of two lion cubs & ought to have bagged one, but dog first rushed at them & then, finding out what they were, ran between my legs & capsized me just as I pulled the trigger. Result a bad miss & some terrible bad language....

....Nakuru is another grand lake, about 9 x 5 miles but unfortunately salt. My cook made my tea with it in the evening & I'm not sure who was most agitated, myself or the cook....The extraordinary point about all these lakes is that large rivers run into them carrying immense volumes of water, but they have no outlet. Evaporation could not possibly account for such vast quantities of water. Though Naivasha, for instance, was apparently about 4ft. above its normal level, the Major tells me that this is about the greatest variation you will ever see. I reckon they must supply the boiler down below.

Near our 10th. camp on Nakuru River, some 8 miles from the Lake, I managed to get a rhino. The old brute was very accommodating, for when I was still a long way from him he sniffed danger, & not knowing which side to look for it, sailed straight down on top of us. The Somalis didn't like it at first but I took them down wind a bit, out of his course & then waited. He came within 100 yds. & then stood to be fired at. I put two successive bullets through behind his shoulder before he knew where he was & then, to oblige me, he started for camp, but had only gone about 300 yds. when he turned round as if to apologise for not being able to go any further & flopped down dead. A grand old bull; meat sufficient for twice my number of men. It was a long way from camp, but when my messenger reached it, the men came flocking out & the fighting over the carcase was a sight to be seen once & never forgotten. However there was a regular Jubilee in camp & all hands were as happy as well-gorged pythons, but it was a job to get them off next morning. There was a heavy white frost on the ground & it was so bitterly cold that I gave them an extra hour by the fires before starting, & having a long march in front of us, we got well roasted long before we got to camp....

....The road for the last two marches up to the Ravine was something too awful. It passes up through glades in the forest between the mountains & was one vast swamp the whole way, up to our knees in black peaty muck. We had to travel slowly & take frequent rests & even then the men were nearly dead at the end of 10 miles & the donkeys only reached camp after dark. The 2nd day the swamps were not so bad but any number of mountain torrents with steep grassy ridges between. This Ravine is a marvellous spot to look at; the camp on the opposite side appears within a stone's throw, but it takes the best part of an hour to get there, & as for the path I think it must have been an old baboon track. The Survey gives the Ravine as 200 ft. broad & 400 ft. deep, so you may imagine it is no mean ditch. In the bottom is a torrent which, at the time I saw it, was romping along at a terrific pace & we had to cross a make-shift bridge Smith had made. It is a lovely place; dense bush & acres of maiden-hair fern & no one could imagine you were right on the Equator in Central Africa. Further up is a grand waterfall coming in from a side stream which drops 150 ft. sheer, & as there was plenty of water, was a glorious sight. The cold at night is deadly, but with such heaps of firewood about, the porters made fires that fairly warmed the whole atmosphere....

....The worst of this march is that there is no food to be had on the road; every lb. has to be carried. Each man carries 10 days rations from here, 15 lbs. wt. which, with a 65 lb. load makes 80 lbs. without his tents &c., a pretty fair weight. Then 10 days food has to be carried either on donkeys or men (donkeys are cheaper) & you have to get through somehow. Any stoppage would mean starvation. In fact many of the new hands will eat their 10 days rations in 3, rather than carry it, & think they can do like the camel does for water for the rest of the time. Then they gorge themselves with meat at the first kill & die gracefully of dysentery a few days later. I had to carry one man in a hammock for five days & then he died, which somewhat annoyed his carriers.

While I was away, de Winton had a taste of what the natives were like, for he had to make three expeditions against them. He managed very well as far as the fighting went, which is an important point here, but he is too quick tempered with the natives & as he doesn't understand a word of any of their languages, this leads to misunderstandings, so they have taken a dislike to him. I had a great reception on my return, for I think they were all beginning to dread that I had gone for good & de Winton was to be left here. I found very good news awaiting me. The Directors are going to send me another man to station at Meranga, at the other end of the District near Kenia, as I recommended. In a very polite & flattering message they also acquainted me with the fact that my salary was increased to 400 Rupees a month from 1st. August, so things so far are very satisfactory....

....de Winton has resigned already & says his salary is not enough for the work, so I am afraid that when the new man comes he will have to stay here for a time until de Winton's place is filled....He is very good company at times, but gets fits of the blues, when he reckons life is not worth living, & I quite agree that if a man was to remain long in that frame of mind it wouldn't be. He hopes to get something better in Nyasaland but I am afraid he won't suit Africa. I have tried to persuade him to stay on here, but he says the pay is not good enough, & certainly 150 tin tokens is none too much, though he may go further & fare worse nowadays....

....My pay now is £100 a year less than the lowest paid man in Uganda Service & this, with all the responsibility attached, is none too grand. Time & circumstances will show me what is best to be done. I certainly have the healthiest locality & the best quarters in East Africa, which is something, but I think the continual strain & anxiety about the natives tells on one pretty heavily & I don't think I could stand it for too long a spell at a time.

Kikuyu. Dec. 22nd 1894

I am writing under difficulties for I am at present laid up in bed through the kindly attentions of a rhino with whom I had an interview on the 11th. As long as the conversation was carried on at 100 yds. range I had decidedly the best of the game, but when the beast entered thoroughly into the spirit of the game, his arguments were so pointed that I was only too glad to be allowed to retire from the game alive. But I must begin from the start & tell you all the details.

Dr. Moffat had arrived here from Uganda on his way to the coast, & as I had heard there were a lot of Wakamba buying slaves among the Wakikuyu, I decided to go down as far as the Athi with him & then to patrol the river & intercept the Wakamba on their way back. On reaching the river we found it flooded & the Doctor was unable to get through & we got rained up there for three days....

....On the morning of the 11th the Doctor got through the river & I started to return here. I met one rhino close to camp but he got away, though badly wounded, & I was very wrath at my bad luck. We had marched about 10 miles, the road terribly muddy & heavy, when I saw my friend close to the road on the open plains & determined to have him. I started off with two men with Sniders, one a Swahili who has been with me ever since I came out, & the other a Somali who unfortunately knows no lingo but his own & turned out anything but useful in the emergency.

Getting to within 100 yds. I put two bullets into the rhino before he shifted quarters, but then he went off at a great rate & we after him, & I managed to get a couple more into him in a very bare place with not even a stone or tuft of grass for cover. This would not have mattered if the men had known what they were about & obeyed my orders. But directly after I had fired, instead of lying down flat while the animal was looking to see where the shot came from, this fool of a Somali blazed off his gun & then left for home.

The old rhino saw the smoke & came down on us full steam ahead. This let the Swahili out too & I was left alone, for I knew it was hopeless to try to run away. I let him come to within 10 yds. & then made a rush to pass by him obliquely, trusting that he would not be able to turn sharp. But he doubled on me like a hare & though I dodged all I knew he was too quick & I soon found myself sailing through space. I no sooner touched ground than I was up & off like a tennis ball, shouting to the men to fire. The rhino obeyed, sharp & fired me up again & hardly let me reach the ground before he repeated the operation. The last time I came down right on my head & was so dazed that I couldn't move & the old beast stood nosing at me viciously but couldn't get his horn into me as I was flat on the ground. So at last he smashed his foot down on my chest twice, which as may be imagined, with about two tons of beef behind it, fairly stove all the breath out of me.

Just as I began to think it was all up, the beast suddenly turned & left me & at the same moment I made a final grand effort in the opposite direction.

Whether he suddenly thought it was time to go & get his own wounds looked after or whether my Swahili managed to hit him with a random shot I don't know, but he left for good & I was jolly glad for I only managed to get a few yards & my legs failed me.

Thank goodness I never lost my senses for a moment, so that when my men came running up expecting to find me dead, I was able to give all the directions at once. I felt rather shaken & was mortally afraid of collapsing any moment, & my men were in such a state of fright that, had I done so, they would not have known what to do, & I should probably have been left to peg out quietly by myself.

As it was, everything went beautifully. I had 30 picked men & 5 went back racing to Machakos for brandy, for I had nothing but a small bottle of champagne here & nothing with me. The cook went on to the river & got some strong coffee ready & a native went to the Fort to fetch a relay of men to help carry. Then I got onto my camp bed & told them to carry me to the Fort whatever happened.

When we got to the river I felt slightly steadier, having got over the worst of the shock, so I took off my clothes to examine damages. I found a beautiful hole through the outside of my left thigh & a terrible bruise just above my ankle on the right leg. This was very painful & I was afraid the small bone of the leg was broken but it has turned out to be only a bruise.

I don't know how the beast managed it, but he tore this right boot, a shooting boot tightly laced, clean off & when the game was over I found I was minus a boot. His horn evidently missed my shin and hooked my boot clean off. The rest of me was little more than a pulp & I couldn't make out where one pain ended & the next commenced.

After tying myself up a bit & arranging the bed fairly comfortably, I had my coffee & then they started for home. They carried me splendidly, though of course it was not exactly a pleasure trip for me, & they only put me down twice in 13 miles. The relief party met us about 4 miles from the Fort & de Winton had sent the champagne which was lucky, for I was getting a bit weary. Then the fresh men rushed me along & I was home before dark.

We ransacked some provision boxes of Major Smith's & found a bottle of whiskey & 1 of port wine, so we were better off than I had hoped. After dressing my wound properly & getting smeared over with Elliman's,[9] I got to sleep & did well considering all things. My chest was very painful but I couldn't feel how many ribs were gone, so I just bandaged them up, but my breathing apparatus was considerably out of order.

The men I sent back to Machakos did some wonderful marching. They had travelled 10 miles with me before the accident happened, then they went back 23 miles to the Doctor's camp & reached there at 1 in the morning. He gave them 2 hours to feed & then loosed them back at 3 a.m., reaching here at 11 at night, 38 miles. So these chaps had no sleep & very little food & marched 71 miles in 38 hours over a very heavy muddy road.

It was awfully good of the Doctor to come back, for he had a sore foot & had to march in slippers, but he is a grand chap & sticks at nothing in that way. He soon sorted out my damages. The most troublesome, though not dangerous, are two ribs which have been smashed off the breast-bone on the right side & stove in. These will take some time to get right & are a general nuisance, for I can't get a long breath, & a sneeze or a cough gives me fits. Thanks to being in splendid health my thigh wound is healing beautifully, but it keeps me in bed at present. I hope to be able to toddle around again in a week or so.

The Doctor reckons the shock alone would have killed most men but thank goodness I am not easily shocked. I attribute my marvellous escape chiefly to a pair of leather breeches I was wearing. These being very loose & strong turned the beast's horn slightly so that he never got a straight fair dig. One dig went through the right leg of my breeches & through the inside of the left leg, bruising the flesh badly, but the point of the horn never entered the flesh. Had it done so he would have got the artery & I should have been done for. There is not much left of these breeches but I intend to fix them up somehow, they served me so well. Some of the thrusts must have been very near shaves, for he hooked the watch pocket off my belt & tore my shirt without wounding me. The whole thing was very marvellous & I can thank God I got off as well as I did.

The Doctor stayed six or seven days with me but I was getting on so well that at last I managed to persuade him to leave on the 19th. This will just enable him to catch his boat by marching hard, as he would otherwise lose a month of his leave....

....De Winton went up with the caravan on 15th. so I am now all alone, but I am praying that my new Assistant, who has just come from home, will get here before Xmas Day, for he is carrying up my load of Xmas luxuries & until he arrives I have nothing but the eternal fat mutton for a feast. He ought to be here on 24th. but if he doesn't arrive I shall have my Xmas alone & in bed, so that it won't be a Jubilee day altogether.

I could really move about a bit now & would much like to, but the

Doctor says if I go fooling around, the wound may suppurate & lay me up for months, so I prefer to stick it out for the present. I am terribly weary of it, for my bed is not exactly a feather one. I have to lie flat on my back, for my ribs object on my right side & my leg on my left, or else get propped up in a sitting position in which I can't sleep. It is pretty uncomfortable. However I might have been lying alongside poor old Nelson, so I mustn't grumble.

Notes

1. The Watt family settled at Ngeleni, eight miles from the fort at Machakos. Stuart Watt imported eucalyptus and wattle trees from Australia and established a fruit farm, growing apples, apricots, plums, quinces and lemons. He won first prize for fruit at the second Agricultural and Horticultural show in Nairobi, February 1903.
2. Francis Hall's cousin.
3. The Laibon or chief medicine man of the Maasai and spokesman for the tribe.
4. Dr. Robert Moffatt. Initially attached to the Scottish Mission at Kibwezi, he was a member of the British Mission to Uganda in 1893 and was later Senior Medical Officer in Uganda.
5. Kamba country, the home of the Wakamba.
6. A proposed colony of a few dozen Europeans who planned to settle on the slopes of Mt. Kenya. They were inspired by the writings of a Viennese economist named Theodor Hertzka who dreamed of a society "that will guarantee to everybody the full and entire produce of his work by the unlimited maintenance of his right to do as he pleases." Not surprisingly the enterprise failed. The colonists travelled as far as Lamu where they drank all their funds and attempted to convert the ladies of the island to their principles of free love. Most returned to Europe.
7. Afrikaans word for a stiff, springy, thin whip made from rhinoceros hide.
8. Ardeotis Kori. The Great African Bustard.
9. Elliman's Ointment used for the relief of muscular aches & pains.

Map 5   Distribution of the major tribes. British East Africa, 1892.

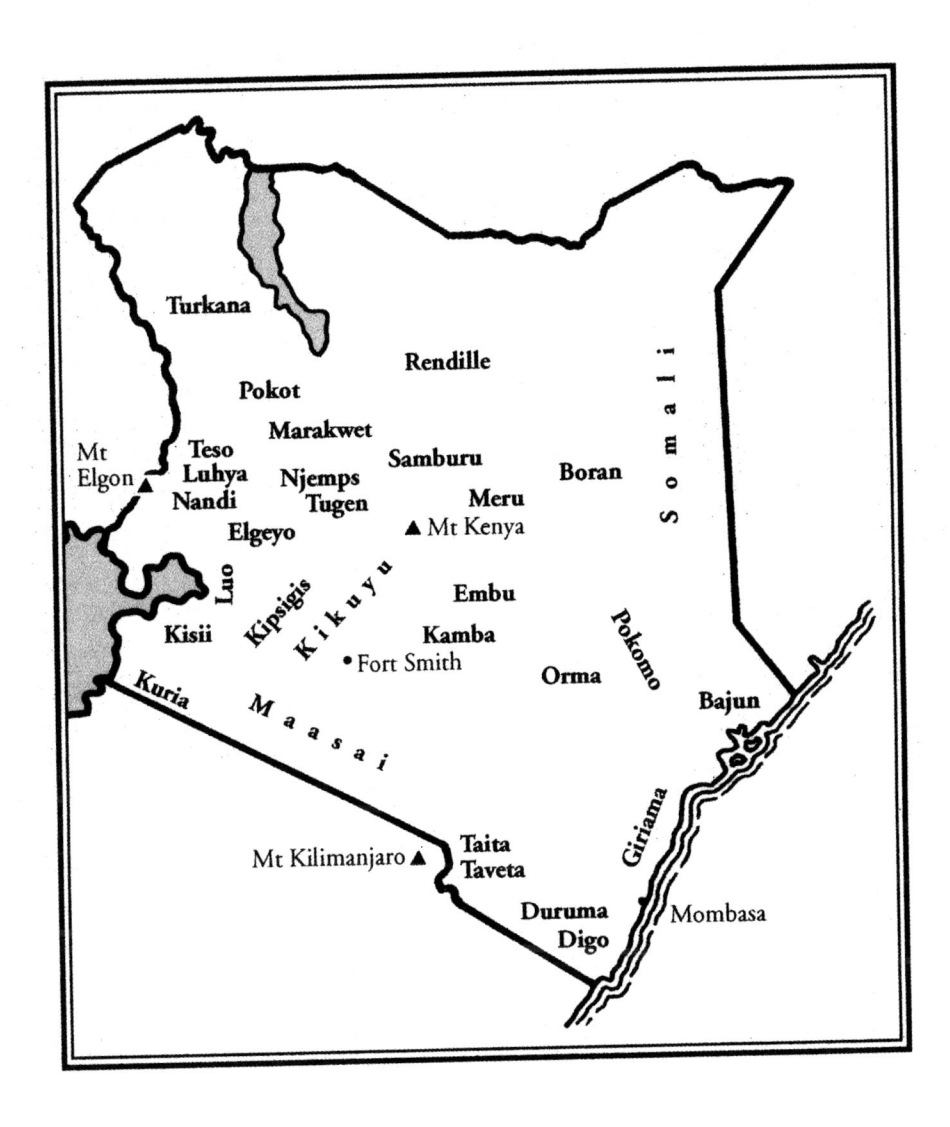

Chapter 4

ATTACKED BY A LEOPARD

Kikuyu. Jany. 12th '95

Just a few lines to let you know that I am jogging along alright. I'm not exactly lively on my pins yet, but manage to knock around a little by the aid of a crutch, & though my chest still gives me a reminder occasionally, it is better than expected. My wound has almost healed up & I have generally made a splendid recovery.

At present it is just as well that I can move about, for we are inundated with caravans. On the 9th there were 1050 men of various caravans camped here & 8 of us Europeans sat down to dinner. My new Assistant, Russell,[1] arrived here on Xmas Eve & brought my supplies of luxuries from the coast, so after all we had a grand feed including plum pudding & mince pie. I was not able to get up for it but had my share of the good things though I was an invalid. De Winton returned on 31st. so we were all three here to see the Old Year out & New one in, & did so in real good style. De Winton left for the coast on 10th. & talks of going to Nyasaland, coffee planting, but I'm afraid he won't do much good.

Russell comes from Halliford-on-Thames & appears to be a very good sort & keen on the work. Poor John Ainsworth has got saddled with a second edition of Schiff for an Asst., named Lane,[2] & is deploring his hard luck. Major Smith is here again en route for Uganda with Dr. Mackinnon[3] & Bagge,[4] both of whom were lately in Coy's service, & a Capt. Ternan,[5] all for Uganda. They leave again on 15th. & then we shall settle down to the old routine again for a month or so....

....I have had a chat with the Major on things in general & he tells me it is unlikely that the Govt. will take over just yet. I have put in my application for leave in June, though I'm not at all sure it will be granted, but I hope it will, for I should immensely like to get home to see you all & I could then get back here in time for any movement that the Coy. might think of making later on. Things appear at present to be in a state of stagnation & I think I had better avail myself of the chance now or I might find myself in for another three or five years service without a trip home....

....I shall try to get Russell thoroughly into the work so that my absence for six months would not mean any change, for he could easily manage the show for that time.

Kikuyu. Feby. 15th '95

I was reckoning that you can only have heard of my smash up about 10 days ago. It seems very absurd to think that by the time you first hear of it, I am out & about again & perfectly recovered. I feel as well as ever now, though I have not quite got my strength back as yet, but when I can get a chance to go away for a few days for some exercise, I shall be quite set up.

Russell has left today for the Eldama Ravine, his first trip, & I hope he will enjoy it. He is a very nice chap, always happy & jolly, & takes kindly to the work. So I hope he will be capable of taking charge during my absence, which would be preferable to having a new man who might not carry things on my particular lines. I hear my application for leave has gone home & I hope it will be granted....

....I have had very bad luck lately with my pets. The jackal got away one night; the boy didn't fasten up the cage. One of my three antelopes died of cold, & three white tailed mongooses died within a fortnight, the last being killed one night by red ants. Two Thomsonii antelopes are getting on beautifully & I hope to get them home to the Zoo. Billy, the male, has a playful knack of prodding the natives on their bare legs, thereby costing me sundry strings of beads as salve for the wounds, but he is a lovely beast & as quiet as can be with me. One baboon is now so big that I have a heavy chain on him, but he is very tame, & beyond getting loose occasionally & raiding the kitchen of everything from a leg of mutton to a tomato, does no harm & affords heaps of fun. When he is loose I hunt him with the dogs; they only play with him & rush him round until he is tired, & when someone tells me he is tired I stroll out & catch him & he is again made prisoner. My crested guinea fowl is still the solitary representative of his kind in the menagerie. I would have had many more, but the natives tie their legs so badly when they catch them, that they can never walk again, so soon die. My menagerie & museum are noted features of the Station....

....Your & Min's remark re the new vicar amused me immensely. I should think from all accounts he would not be very popular. I have never had the chance, & don't hanker after it, of meeting his son, but have heard a good deal of him from Uganda men. The Universal opinion seems to be that he is an "unmitigated ass." He must be pretty awful if he beats some of the Missionary bounders I know up there, but they say there is only one man to beat him, a lunatic called Pilkington, who swears that he found the Holy Ghost on one of the Sesse Islands. This nearly killed Colville, for he made such a point of reporting the matter at headquarters that Colville couldn't get rid of him, & all hands speak of him now as the "Holy Ghost Man."

These infernal Missionaries do more to bring religion into ridicule than all the atheists & sinners that ever lived. The hypocrisy of the thing is very clearly brought home to me as I write this, for there is a caravan camped outside carrying over 100 loads, 65 lbs. each, of goods, provisions &c. for the Uganda Missionaries. These loads cost £8 each for carriage from Mombasa to Uganda, paid out of C.M.S. funds, & then these men pretend that they are labouring for God on a bare living, & poor deluded people at home support them in a luxury that I for one could not afford. Personally there are a few good, honest, conscientious men amongst Missionaries, but as a rule these men, like poor little Charters of Kibwezi, are generally to be found amongst the representatives of any church but our own....

....We cut our first cucumber the other day. Purkiss tried to grow them but they failed, & I found the old gardener had a few seeds stuck away somewhere. These were put in & we have now 7 or 8 good cucumbers. I didn't tell the Major when he passed, as they were not ready, but shall be able to astonish him when he returns.

Kikuyu. March 14th '95

I have been praying for the mail to arrive in good time so that I could get any news there was before writing, as I heard there was a good chance of things being settled between the Govt. & the Coy. It is now 10 p.m. & the mail has just arrived, & as I leave at daybreak for Ravine, I have not much time for writing....I feel perfectly fit & look forward to the trip, but have to see how my leg stands hard work. I am taking two riding donkeys in case I get knocked up, but hope I shall not have to mount them. It is pouring with rain night & day, so I shall not have a very pleasant time of it, but one of us must go, or the caravan might bust up, & as Russell only got back the other day, I cannot expect him to go again....He has thoroughly settled down to life here & enjoys it & is first class company & energetic. We get on splendidly, & since my small stock of energy is soon exhausted, a little new blood does good....

....The lions are playing up old gooseberry on the road at one camp no less than 7 men have been taken during the last month or two. One of Russell's men was sleeping between the tent & the fire, inside the ring of tents, & the lion whipped him off. I hope to get this beast with a trap gun this trip....

....I have had a distinguished visitor in the shape of Count d'Harnoncourt, an Austrian, on a shooting trip. He is an awfully nice fellow & stayed with me 4 days. He is so delighted that he intends to return here next year & make his headquarters here & at Machakos. I have bought a "Mannlicher," the Austrian magazine rifle, so shall now have a good spare one to back me up instead of the Snider which the men carry & which will not pierce a rhino or elephant. I don't know how my nerves will serve me after my shake up, but as my "Mannlicher" fires point blank up to 500 yds. (I have tried it at a target) I shall be able to choose my own distance from a rhino. But I shall still stick to my old love, the Martini. I know what it can do....

....I have heard nothing about my leave as yet, & of course have the right, if things appear favourable, to accept or refuse it as I may feel inclined. You may be sure I know when I have got hold of a good thing, & bad as the pay is, the Station & the District are not to be equalled in Africa, & rather than run the risk of losing it in favour of some toy Brigadier General of the Guards or such like, I would forego my leave, much as I look forward to it. Kikuyu, I find, tells on one pretty considerably & one can't keep up full steam all the time without feeling the effects. One can face battle, murder & sudden death for a short period, but one day will probably lose the game &

go under. It is just as well to make the most of a chance of a holiday when one gets it, provided it is not permanent....

....I have far more medical & surgical work than I can attend to properly, & though I have been wonderfully lucky with surgical cases, wounds, fractures &c., I have lost lots of good men from diseases of various kinds which I know nothing about. I have made frequent appeals for a Doctor, for 400 men is too much of a handful, but the Coy. can't afford it. And the Masai are always getting damaged some way or other, giving me plenty of work at all hours....One of my askaris has just had a fit, so I have had an unexpected interruption.

Kikuyu. April 24th. '95

My dear Dad,

Just a few lines in pencil to let you know that I am not quite dead, though pretty bad. The cause of all my troubles this time was a leopard which managed to get a couple of teeth into my knee, poisoning it so badly that I have been nearly dead. Luckily Dr. Ansorge was going to Uganda, so I have had medical aid & he is still with me & intends to see me through. He performed an operation on my knee two days ago which appears to have done worlds of good & now I am getting along very fairly. This is writing under difficulties, so I must close. With best love to all.

Letter from Edward Russell to Colonel Hall

Fort Smith, Kikuyu. 24 April '95

Dear Sir,

Your son has asked me to write to tell you of his present condition. I must regret that I am unable to say more than that he is in a very precarious condition still, but infinitely better than before the operation was performed on his knee three days ago by Dr. Ansorge. Both the Doctor & myself have hopes of his ultimate recovery which however cannot be for some weeks to come. Dr. Ansorge has very kindly consented to stay here until all danger has passed & I have but little doubt that with careful nursing, which you may rest assured he will get, and good feeding, your son will pull round and, before many weeks have passed, will be in a fit condition to leave for the coast en route for home.

Letter from Edward Russell to Mr. G.S. Mackenzie

Kikuyu. April 24 '95

Before the mail-bag closes I will write to you to tell you about poor old Hall who is lying here in a very critical condition. On the 17th of last month he was slightly bitten in the knee by a leopard and so poisonous was this bite that by midnight his knee had swollen to quite double its normal size & gave him such intense pain as to make him quite delirious and he remained in this state for about 12 days. About 22 days after the accident, the rhino wound he sustained last December burst open and so found a good outlet for the accumulated matter which relieved the thigh greatly but not the knee.

On the 13th of this month Dr. Ansorge arrived and last Sunday 21st, assisted by Capt. Pulteney, Lane, and myself, put Hall under chloroform and operated on the knee, an operation lasting an hour and a quarter. Whether the poor fellow will ultimately pull through remains to be seen. Personally I am inclined to think he will as he has such a wonderful pluck, but the Dr., who is still here, is doubtful.

For the first twelve days I had a very hard time, what with nursing frequently right through the night, besides having to attend to the ordinary business up here. At the expiration of that time however, Gilkie[6] came up from Machakos to help me, staying a week or so, and when he returned he sent Lane up, who is a capital nurse.

Letter from Capt. N.P. Pulteney to Mr. J. Le Fleming Jr.[7]

Kedong River, Kikuyu. 23-4-95

Dear Le Fleming,

It is sometime since we met, but was reminded of you & many pleasant recollections by Hall at Kikuyu, whose guest I was last Saturday & Sunday. I found Hall in bed suffering from a leg, the blood of which had been poisoned by the bite of a leopard below the knee. He had been lying in bed for over 20 days before the Dr. Ansorge came up on his way to Uganda. The leg had swollen to a tremendous size but at last found a vent in his thigh through his old rhino wound, the matter having to travel quite 15 inches. It was with the greatest difficulty he was dressed daily; his knee gave him such excruciating pain & he was covered with bed sores. Before the Dr. arrived he was looked after by Mr. Russell night & day in an unselfish & worthy way which cannot be too highly praised. Neither of them knew anything about medicine & their stores were limited. Of course the wound ought to have been opened a fortnight before, but as it was, I thoroughly agreed with the Doctor that the only chance was an operation.

The operation took place on Sunday afternoon at 4.20 p.m. & lasted an hour & 20 minutes. Hall took a tremendous lot of chloroform but was quite peaceful & talked but little. After he was once off, I undertook the chloroform and Russell & Lane helped the Doctor. The operation was well done, but disclosed his leg to be in such a fearful state that I am afraid there is but little chance of his ever recovering. The tissues had all rotted away from the bone & a piece of bone fully an inch long was dead. The tube was successfully put through & worked satisfactorily before he came to. His only chance is his extraordinary constitution & if he can pull through the next week he might have a chance as the piece of bone might come away. But I am afraid that he has been too long ill to be strong enough. Had he not been in such a terrible state of weakness, his leg should have come off at the thigh, but in his condition it was out of the question & I am sure the Doctor did all he could.

Personally I had to continue my way to Uganda the next morning & therefore cannot know how he fares for a long time. I trust that you will treat this letter as private & not create alarming news about him until you hear something definite. But having had many kindnesses from your hand formerly, I thought you would like to know what is written, and if poor Hall is spared to see you again, you can show him the letter & light your pipes with it.

Letter from Francis Hall to his father, Colonel Hall.

Kikuyu. May 16th '95

I am still in bed though getting along fairly well. My leg is the only worry & that is healing nicely, though at times gives me awful fits just now. After being dressed in the morning I howl my lungs out while the nerves & sinews are arranging themselves. Bed sores have been a frightful complication as I have to be lifted daily to get at those on my back, but thank God these are nearly finished, only one tiny spot remains, but this means lifting & the subsequent agonies.

They have only today altered our Mail Time Table & I am writing in haste to let you know my plans. First, if I am fit to travel, of which I think there need be no doubt, Major Smith is going to take me down to Mombasa, leaving here about 12th June, & I hope to catch the Brit. Indian boat which leaves Mombasa on 9th July. This takes me to Aden where I tranship to the P&O & go straight to London Docks. The P&O should reach home about the first week in August, but Jack will be able to find out at their offices. I don't know whether I shall be a cripple or an invalid, but I hope someone will come to meet me at the docks. If I happen to miss that boat at Mombasa, I will cable "Hall Tonbridge England Missed." I shall then have to wait a month but I hope this will not happen. As it is I shall be a month later than I hoped, but I am not fit to travel yet, so can't help it.

I have entirely regained my bodily strength, but the Doctor appears to have hacked my knee about so much that the thing takes a long time healing & we have to keep the exterior wounds open in case of any fresh deposit forming inside. I have had a terrible time of it, & you may imagine was very nearly visiting my Creator, for Russell sent an express to Machakos to borrow a Prayer Book to read the service over me. The Doctor also said he didn't think I would live, but I'm jogging along very well for a dead man; they didn't know the Hall constitution. Still it has tried me terribly & I have completely lost all my nerves & pluck now the worst is over, so I suffer more than I otherwise should. However it can't last for ever & I can thank God it is no worse. It is now 9 weeks since it happened, so I shall probably complete my three months in bed. I have my leg straight in a splint, so that if it remains stiff it will at least be straight, & I shall probably be able to get it fixed right at home. The Doctor did not stay long after the operation but Russell is a grand nurse & looks after me like a mother. I also have Lane up here, the other new man who came up to Machakos & he is also awfully good. Luckily for me, when I first came in, he had a fair supply of things & also had in store some champagne belonging to Govt. & port wine & other things belonging to Major Smith. Of course in African style the Major placed all his at my disposal & by giving the stingy old Doctor a receipt, we got the Govt. champagne. This & the contributions from passing friends kept me going; in fact I was awfully lucky in every way....

....We have all received our three months' notice from the Coy. up to 30th. June, but I have already had a good offer from the best private firm out here to do their transport work & also heard that the Govt. will keep us on, & privately, that I shall probably be retained here. So there is no fear of want of employment, but I shall have to see to these matters at the coast before I leave, & try to make all right for my return.

Letter from Mr. J.R.W. Pigott to Colonel Hall.

Mombasa. 8 June '95.

Dear Sir,

I received your telegram asking about your son & have just sent you the following telegram "Much better has written." The mail from up country arrived this morning and as I see he has written to you, it is not necessary for me to go into particulars. I need not say how sincerely glad I am to be able to send you such a good report, as apart from personal feelings of friendship, I consider your son a most excellent and valuable officer & should be very sorry if anything were to happen to deprive the country of his services.

We are longing to hear when the country is to be transferred; the present state of suspense is bad for all concerned, especially for the country itself. I think it is high time that the present Government at home made room for their betters. Excuse a hurried note written amid constant interruptions, this being mail day.

Letters from Francis Hall to his father.

Kikuyu. June 16th '95,

After all I am still here & consequently cannot possibly catch the July boat. However we leave here next Thursday 20th. for Mombasa & hope to get down in 20 days at most. I shall have plenty of time then to rest & pick up before the August boat leaves. I was getting along so slowly here & my leg seemed to get very little better, so I wrote through a friend of mine to the new Doctor who had just come to the Mission at Kibwezi, halfway between here & Mombasa, & he, like a brick, started off at once & came as quick as he could. He is quite a young chap, just fresh from Edinburgh, but very nice & as careful as he can be. His presence alone eased my mind & after the first few days a visible improvement took place in my leg. Then the dear old Major turned up (Smith) & he of course is a grand one to cheer one up.

Altogether things have gone well & now that all is ready for a start, I begin to think my recovery is within measurable distance. Everyone has been only too good. I wrote to the coast for a large order; 2 cases of port wine, 1 champagne & a case of other medical comforts, which in all would cost about £25 to deliver here, & of course intended to pay it for myself, but the Administrator, Pigott, got hold of it & charged it all to the Coy. & wrote me an awfully nice letter about it.

Russell of course is still nursing me like a hospital nurse. He sleeps in my room & is at my beck & call day & night. Thank goodness Gilkison, my locum tenens, has arrived, & like a good chap has given Russell leave to go to Mombasa with me. The Doctor is also going to see me all the way down, & as I have 20 picked men to carry my stretcher, I have the best possible chance of a fairly comfortable journey.

Russell has made me a regular swagger palanquin; canvas & bamboos for the stretcher & a fairly soft moss mattress to cover it. This is slung on ropes to a long bamboo which two men shoulder. The porters absolutely can't walk any other way than single file, so one has to arrange a stretcher accordingly. Over the top bamboo, & let into the sides of the stretcher, is a light framework covered with canvas, with side curtains &c. The whole of this top lifts off so as to enable them to lift me in or out should they require to do so. Everything has been thought of to ease my journey & by the aid of

God & with a change of air, I ought not only to stand it well but also pick up on the journey.

With ordinary luck I hope to get away by the Brit. India boat which leaves Mombasa on 6th August. By that time I ought to be able to use my leg a little to move about....

....The Wakikuyu Headmen were all called in the other day to say goodbye & be introduced to Gilkison. They all said they were sorry to lose me & begged I would come back quickly. Then one old man got up & offered up a prayer for my speedy recovery & return, the whole mob joining in a sort of chorus. It was very impressive & if they were half as sincere as they seemed, they would be glad to see me back. The fact is we have got into each other's ways & thoroughly understand each other & they are very frightened of getting a new man who would upset everything & start them all fighting again. However G. has got orders to carry on as usual, so I hope things will go well....

....Russell is in a great fever now, for he is afraid you will think he frightened you unnecessarily in his first account of me. But the fact was I was so nearly dead that had he told the whole truth it would have been worse. He is a first rate chap & one of the first things I shall do at home is to go & see his people & tell them how good he has been.

East African Scottish Mission; Kibwezi. June 29th. '95

I have already written one letter by this mail, but as we have got ahead of the mail men I must just drop a line to let you know that I have come so far safely & am improving rapidly, thanks to the Doctor's care. I am travelling in great comfort for this part of the world. I have a splendid stretcher with a fairly soft moss mattress & a splendid canvas awning with side curtains, all lined with coloured cloth to keep out glare. The whole thing is very comfortable & carries easily, & as I have 20 picked men to carry me in relays of fours, I get along well.

The Doctor & Russell are with me & I am fairly supplied with all I want. I have enough champagne to allow me a pint bottle a day to Mombasa, besides brandy & port wine. I eat like a horse & am picking up wonderfully. Since I started on the journey I have been able to sleep well without the aid of sleeping draughts; in fact there is such an improvement in me, both bodily & "legly," that friends on the road rather fancy I'm a bit of a fraud & their sympathy has been wasted. We have now, thank goodness, passed over the worst of the road. It has been simply terrible, & for the first few days while I was still weak & nervous, I had an awful time of it. In many places it took the whole 20 men to pass me along by hand, & what with mountains & rivers, they had no easy task. We have come along very well, having done 160 miles in 9 days. Today we are resting here to allow the Doctor to get his things together & give me a rest, & we have 190 miles to do to Mombasa which will take us 11 days....Here comes the Doctor to dress my leg, so no more peace for the present. The ordinary dressing does not pain much nowadays, I am so much better, but occasionally he has to make a fresh cut & then get beans. Well I hope to be home by the August boat to see you all & that I shall be passably fit by then.

Extract from the "Zanzibar Gazette" August 1895.

Mr. A. Hall (sic) is lying in hospital at Mombasa having been brought down by bearers on a stretcher from Kikuyu....

....Unexpectedly one day a huge leopard went straight for him after receiving a shot and Mr. Hall, not having time to reload, broke its advance by holding his gun across his body, catching the leopard's open jaw. Then came a struggling of life and death, Mr. Hall trying to strangle it and his boy bravely joining in the attempt. They were successful after a terrible contest but Mr. Hall was gashed from head to foot and presented a ghastly appearance on being carried in to Kikuyu, one knee especially receiving fearful injuries.

LETTER FROM FRANCIS HALL TO HIS FATHER.

Mombasa. Aug. 1st. '95

It is a terrible disappointment to me not being allowed to leave by this mail. but as the Doctor says I had better not risk it, I must make up my mind to wait another month. I have picked up wonderfully since I arrived & am now quite strong & well.

The numerous holes in my leg have nearly all healed, but two of my bed-sores are still obstinate & these are really what are keeping me back. I am still in bed, but the Doctor expects me to be about on crutches in a week's time, & by the next mail I shall be able to look after myself a little. There is fluid on the knee making it quite stiff. This I shall have to get fixed up in a London Hospital & whether it will be too late, & the leg remains stiff or not, remains to be seen. However I must put up with it whether it comes right or not.

My recovery has fairly astonished all the Doctors who have seen my leg & they reckon the journey from Kikuyu to the coast in my then state a marvellous performance. We reached Mombasa from Kikuyu, 350 miles in 19 days, & the men carried me splendidly the whole way. Our procession, as one of the Missionaries said, was one of the most curious Hospital parties ever seen. About 15 of the men, dressed in Masai kit & armed with spears, raved & danced in front & most effectually cleared the road. Then came my regal palanquin surrounded by some of the fellows who came out to meet us (thoughtfully equipped with bottled beer). Behind me came the drummers trying who could beat the loudest & about 100 men carrying the loads & yelling with 10 h.p. lungs & all the population of Mombasa joining in chorus. The Major came in about an hour later with his 250 men who, of course, made even more noise, so the place was pretty lively.

I found things ready for me in the hospital & have since been a prisoner in a very nice airy room looking straight over the sea in front, & down the harbour on the left. There are two large ventilators, besides three doors & two windows, so that by opening the lot I can manage to keep fairly cool, though for the first few days I felt the heat terribly. I still have a splendid appetite & am almost too fat, though the feeding in Mombasa, with the exception of fish & beer, is not nearly as good as in Kikuyu....

....As to my status here, I asked the C.G. [Consul-General] who I belonged to at present, & he didn't seem to be quite sure. However the Govt. are paying all the expenses here & Pigott tells me I shall get my passage from either the Coy. or the Govt. As to the future, the C.G. said, "Oh, you are all right; you needn't worry about that!" & asked me if I should like to go back to Kikuyu & of course I said "you bet." So the present arrangement is that Russell stays there alone in charge until I come back, Gilkie being required for a coast Station & the C.G. said, "Go home & get fit, & come out again as soon as you can."

So things are all going very well, & even a stiff leg wouldn't prevent my being able to carry on in Kikuyu as before. The C.G. is coming here again in a few days & when I get home I shall be able to tell you more about the scheme for running this new Protectorate.

Notes

1. Edward J.H. Russell. IBEA Company.

2. Charles Robert William Lane. Assistant Collector, Machakos

3. Dr. A.D. Mackinnon CMG. Accompanied F.J. Jackson on his safari from the coast to Lake Victoria in 1890.

4. Stephen Salisbury Bagge CMG. Member of Captain Lugard's expedition to Uganda in 1890, he witnessed the signatures of Lugard and the Kabaka, Mwanga, to the treaty of March 1892.

5. Captain (later Brig. General) Trevor Patrick Breffney Ternan CB CMG DSO. Following a distinguished military career in Egypt and Sudan he joined the Uganda Rifles in 1894, becoming Commandant in 1897. Appointed Commissioner and Consul-General of Uganda Protectorate in 1897 and held the same post in British East Africa in 1900. He built Fort Ternan, forty miles east of Lake Victoria, to protect travellers and surveyors.

6. Thomas Train Gilkison. Briefly took over command of Fort Smith during Hall's illness. Subsequently Superintendent of Shipping and Customs 1895.

7. Jack Le Fleming, Francis Hall's brother in-law.

Fort Smith, Kikuyu, with Major Smith's caravan camped in the foreground. Francis Hall's house with chimney is to the right of the flag pole. Photograph taken by John Ainsworth Feb,1895.

1898 at Fort Smith
Standing: H.C.E. Barnes, F.G.Hall, Mr. McPherson, C.W.Hobley,
Sitting: Mrs. Hobley, John Ainsworth, Mrs. Ainsworth, L.E. Caine
In front: Judge Cator

Fort Smith
Standing: Billy (pet Thomson's Gazelle), Mr. D'Silva, Mr. Kitchen, Capt. F S Dugmore
Sitting: Mr. C R W Lane, Mrs James Martin, Francis Hall
Infront: James Martin

D'Silva was Mrs Martin's cousin; Mr Kitchen managed Smith Mackenzie's farm at Dagoretti; Capt. Dugmore commanded Ngong Fort and was later tried for murder. Charles Lane was assistant collector at Machakos.

Fort Smith
Standing: Dr. Ansorge, Francis Hall, Major Eric Smith
Sitting: Major Roddy Owen, James Martin

Dr. Ansorge operated on Francis Hall's knee after the leopard mauling. Major Smith lost an arm while fighting in in Sudan and is skilfully concealing the fact. Major Owen was posted in Uganda and James Martin prospered as a colourful caravan leader and illiterate administrator.

FORT SMITH. April 1899.

F.G.H.   The late   The late
Sir Frederick Jackson.   Sir Ernest Berkeley.   Major (later Col.)   Mr. Snowden.
                                                                   (Uganda Rlwy.)
         Mrs. Snowden.   Mrs. Boedeker.   A.E. Smith.
                                                  C.R.L. Lane.

Photo taken by Dr. Boedeker. The weighing scales in the background recorded the
weights of everybody who signed the Fort's Visitors Book.

Kikuyu women bringing firewood to a caravan camped at Fort Smith.

Kinyanjui, Chief of the Wakikuyu near Fort Smith was a great friend of Francis Hall.

Building the Uganda Railway from Mombasa to Lake Victoria.

The man-eating lion which snatched Supt. Ryall from a railway carriage at Kima and ate him. See note following Chapter 10.

Panorama of Nairobi taken from the District Engineer's house in 1899.

Kikuyu Railway Station is about three miles from Fort Smith. The Railway climbs from Nairobi towards the Kikuyu escarpment before plunging into the Great Rift Valley.

Francis Hall's grave in the centre of Muranga town.

Chapter 5

CONVALESCENCE IN ENGLAND

AUGUST 1895 - JUNE 1896.

Three months after Francis Hall left Mombasa, a massacre and the death of a white man occurred in his area of jurisdiction which was to have an important effect on European relationships with the Maasai. It is also fair to say that if Hall had been present the incident would never have happened.

In the first week of November 1895, Thomas Gilkison, in temporary command of Fort Smith during Francis Hall's absence, despatched a food caravan of some 1,150 men to Ravine. It consisted of 150 Swahilis, fifty of them armed with Snider carbines and about 1,000 Kikuyu porters. Gilkison appointed a young and inexperienced Swahili to lead the caravan and sent no European in command. This was contrary to standard practice and unheard of with a caravan of that size. The outward journey to Ravine was completed without incident but on the way back some Swahilis and Kikuyus stole milk from a Maasai manyatta near Kijabe and attempted to persuade several Maasai women to go with them to their camp. It is unclear whether the men committed these acts of folly on their own initiative or were under orders from their headman. Whatever the case, a senior Maasai moran visited the headman of the caravan and warned him to keep his men under control.

Next morning, November 26th, the caravan struck their tents at four o'clock and passed by the same manyatta on the way to Fort Smith.

Demonstrating his ignorance of the Maasai, and despite the warning of the previous day, the Swahili headman ordered the seizure of some young girls for his pleasure and a party of armed Swahilis went to do his bidding. In the inevitable confrontation that followed, an askari fired his Snider and from that moment the caravan was doomed. The rifle shot alerted neighbouring manyattas so that the outraged Maasai were quickly reinforced. In the dark before dawn the Elmoran swooped vengefully on the raiders and then turned on the unarmed porters whose only hope was instant flight. The Maasai pursued the porters down the Kedong Valley and speared all they could find. 540 Kikuyu porters were killed, 86 Swahilis, 13 Swahili askaris, 6 Kikuyu headmen and 1 Swahili headman, total 646. Maasai losses were less than forty until a Scots accountant arrived on the scene to balance the books.

Andrew Dick was the IBEA Company's first Chief Accountant in Mombasa, an irascible man and a rebel by nature. After two years' efficient service he was dismissed from the Company on some flimsy pretext and Dick proceeded to embarrass his former employers whenever the opportunity occurred. With the help of Smith Mackenzie, the trading company, he set himself up as a trader and acquired a five year concession on generous terms at Mumia's and Ravine along the Uganda road. His ambition was to establish a chain of stores along the caravan route and he succeeded in establishing eleven. "Trader Dick" was a quarrelsome, hot tempered, sometimes violent man, who was given to thrashing the natives and generally dispensing summary justice as he saw fit. He was warned officially at least once about this tendency to take the law into his own hands.

At the time of the massacre he was camped a day's march from Fort Smith and met survivors of the massacre who recounted their version of events. Instinctively he took the part of the apparent victims and without bothering to verify their story, prepared to exact retribution from the Maasai. First he sent a runner to Fort Smith requesting an escort and Gilkison responded by sending a Sergeant with thirty soldiers and instructions not to proceed to the Kedong Valley. Incongruously, Gilkison also sent three French hunters who had stayed the previous night at Fort Smith and wished to proceed through the troubled region. With the reluctant and largely non-combatant help of the Frenchmen, Dick captured 200 head of cattle and many sheep and donkeys. In the act of driving off the livestock, Dick and a handful of soldiers became separated. The Maasai regrouped and attacked from all sides. Dick is reported to have killed between forty and a hundred Maasai warriors single handed in a last ditch stand before either running out of ammunition or suffering a weapon jam. For a time he may have kept the Maasai at bay by raising and aiming his useless Remington rifle, but eventually a warrior named Ole Lekutit killed him from behind. The Frenchmen witnessed the spear thrust through the ribs and heart that killed Dick instantly but they were unable to recover the body and were forced to withdraw.

By chance the Chief Laibon of the Maasai people, Olonana (Lenana), was making a ceremonial visit to Fort Smith, his first meeting with a European official at a Government outpost. Gilkison feared that the Kikuyu would overwhelm the fort and seize Olonana with his elders. He was also concerned that the food which the Kikuyu supplied for stations further up-country would never again be made available to the Government. He sent a runner to John Ainsworth, Sub-Commissioner at Machakos, and Ainsworth hurried to the scene to make a full enquiry into the last hours of the caravan.

In meetings with the Laibon, his Maasai elders and the Kikuyu elders, Ainsworth first persuaded Olonana to disperse his warriors to their manyattas and to surrender the caravan's captured arms and property. He was then joined by Frederick Jackson from Ravine Fort and when the full story was known they delivered an elegant judgement.

The matter was resolved according to traditional principles of African justice, where all wrongs and grievances are settled by a fine of livestock determined by the elders. Imprisonment was an unknown concept and thought barbaric. The Maasai were not punished, either for the massacre or for the killing of Andrew Dick, on the grounds that the Elmoran had reacted to the gravest provocation. Yet, according to custom, the Kikuyu had to be compensated for the death of their men and therefore the stolen Maasai livestock, which the Frenchmen had driven to Fort Smith, were shared among the families of the dead Kikuyu porters and all parties were satisfied. The Kikuyu elders agreed that the Maasai were not to blame and Olonana reminded his followers of the great Laibon Mbatian's advice that the Maasai should not oppose the newcomers and his prediction that disaster would befall the Maasai and their herds if they killed a white man.

Olonana was surprised and reassured by the just manner in which the tragic incident had been settled. The understanding which existed between himself and Francis Hall was cemented by the settlement and Olonana became a loyal friend of the Government. All roads and routes through Maasailand became safe for even the smallest caravan. Nevertheless, if Francis Hall had been in command of Fort Smith at the time, it is reasonable to say that the caravan would never have been despatched without a European leader and the Kedong massacre would probably never have occurred.

Mbatian was the last Laibon to rule the Maasai before the white men came. He died at Namanga Hill in about 1885. Born in Kisongo and of average height and build, with only one eye, he ruled over all clans and all parts of Masailand with the help of four elders, the chiefs and the warriors. He was a druid or seer and made many prophecies, including the coming of the white man and the Uganda Railway.

It is related that Mbatian called the elders together and told them something white was coming and would bring with it a long snake. "I have tried to stop these people in the sea, but I have failed," he said. The Elmoran replied "let them come and we shall face them," but Mbatian told them they could not fight the white men. He went about picking up war clubs and saying, "let me strike the head of this snake. I cannot find the head of this snake." The Elmoran insisted that the white men should be allowed to come but Mbatian replied, "the white men cannot come in my lifetime. They cannot come while I am the head of the Maasai. If they want to come during the lifetime of Olonana and Senteu (Mbatian's sons) then that is their affair." The Elmoran stated that they wished to defeat the white men in battle and Mbatian replied, "very well, I will allow them to come, and they are coming. But a long snake will cross the country from East to West, with no tail and no head, and as soon as it arrives you will be ruled by uncircumcised people, and they will have a piece of wood with water and fire in it and it will shout and cry as it moves and it will carry people. There it is, I have left it."

When Lord Rosebery's Liberal Government, with a slim majority of 44, was defeated in the House of Commons in a vote on the supply of small arms ammunition, Lord Salisbury's Conservative Government lost no time in deciding that the Uganda Railway should be built. The Uganda Railway Bill was fiercely debated and harshly criticised by Henry Labouchere, the anti-imperialist MP, who said that the railway "started from nowhere and nobody wanted to use it. It went nowhere and nobody wanted to come back by it." Among other things he questioned the capital cost, annual running costs and the suitability of the climate. "All I know is that about 60 percent of the English officers sent there are dead and that those who have come back have come back so utterly ruined in health that they are hardly worth anything." The Uganda Railway Bill was passed on August 1st 1896 and met with no opposition in the Lords.

Once the Conservative party came to power it was a foregone conclusion that the Uganda Railway would proceed. George Whitehouse, the Chief Engineer, and his staff arrived in Mombasa aboard the s.s. Ethiopia in December 1895 and immediately started work to establish a base of operations on the island. He bought 372 acres of land near the natural harbour of Kilindini and built accommodation for the first draft of 2,000 labourers and artisans from India. He built stores, a jetty, hospital facilities, sheds for rolling stock, workshops, a reservoir and a distillery for producing 12,000 gallons of water daily. In April 1896 work started on the temporary wooden viaduct spanning Macupa creek from Mombasa island to the mainland. The 1,732 feet long viaduct was completed in 92 working days despite torrential rain and plate-laying began in earnest towards Lake Victoria, 582 miles away to the North-West, in August 1896.

Meanwhile, in England, Francis Hall spent some time in hospital recovering his health and fitness. A surgical attempt to correct his stiff left knee failed, so that ever afterwards he walked with a limp, and after several weeks he was discharged from hospital to continue his convalescence at home.

As soon as he was strong enough he fulfilled his promise to visit Edward Russell's family at Halliford-on-Thames where he paid his respects and gave testimony to their son's devoted nursing. No doubt Russell had included in his letters home a series of impressions of Francis Hall and it may be surmised that the Russell family was able to form a mental picture of their son's superior. It is even possible that members of the Russell family, including his sister Beatrice, may have visited the wounded hero in hospital, bringing him perhaps a bottle of Robinson's lemon barley water and the latest edition of the Illustrated London News or Punch magazine. Wherever the first meeting took place it seems that there must have been subsequent meetings, for Francis Hall and Beatrice Russell fell in love. Hall spent ten months in England and by the time he sailed for Mombasa, he and Bee had come to an understanding that they would be married in England during his next leave, due in twenty months time.

Chapter 6

BACK IN HARNESS

Mombasa. June 21st '96.

My dear old Dad,
    I hope Bee told you she had heard from me from Aden. I would have written to you too, but it was all I could manage to get through one letter. Aden was simply frightful, the heat day & night was unbearable & it fairly upset us all. We could only lie in long chairs & gasp & curse our fate having to stop there for three days....But the thing which compensated me for all the weary waiting was that I managed to meet Ted[1] after all. His boat was due on Wednesday, & we were to leave on Thursday at 5 a.m., & at 11 p.m. Wed. his boat was not in, so I had to go on board mine. However I chartered a shore boat to stay alongside & waited for the signal guns, & about 1.30 a.m. she came in. I rushed off in my boat & thank goodness caught Ted, & after we had sent his baggage off he came back with me & stayed until our ship sailed, so we had a few hours together. We were both terribly sleepy & I was a wreck next day, but no matter, we met after 16 years.
    When we got round Guardajui we met the full force of the monsoon & as we were in a wretched cockle-shell of a boat, the "Kola" under 500 tons, we got the most awful tossing. She fairly turned upside down & inside out &

so did we all. Even Tritton, an old sailor, was ill & the worst was we couldn't move about; the decks were at all angles & water swilling about all over & the food was something too awful. To have a dish of tripe & onions shoved suddenly under your nose when you were just hesitating between leaving the table or trying to smile blankly through the rest of the meal was too much. I attended every meal but had to leave hurriedly from breakfast once through this....

....Hardinge, the Consul three quarter General sent a note off to the ship when we arrived to ask me to dine with him that night & you may imagine my surprise at meeting no less than 5 ladies there. We had a very jolly party & the next night we all met again at the Sub. Commrs.'s house....Rogers, Sub. Commr. of Lamu, whose place I was to have taken, is remaining there so I have to go on special service to Mweli,[2] the place where all the fighting has been going on, to place matters generally on a sound footing. The row is over now & the Govt. has granted an amnesty to all the smaller fry of the rebels, permitting them to return to the country & settle down after being disarmed. I am to go there, establish a sort of township as a centre under a native Akida, & boss things up generally. There may be some kudos attached to it, I hope there is, but I would far rather go straight back to Kikuyu....We were to have left tomorrow, but I got a wire not to leave until the C.G. comes up tomorrow as he wishes to see me. I only hope he changes his plans & sends me off sharp to Kikuyu.

Tomorrow the mail returns from Zanzibar, & as Hardinge is going home by it, there are to be great functions. At 9 a.m. the Indian residents present an address; at 11 we Protectorate Officers give him a dinner, or rather lunch; at 4 p.m. more addresses, & as I have to dine out in the evening, I hope to get an hour's peace after this. The Doctor is very kindly giving me a room in the hospital so I am in the best of quarters.

All the fellows here are awfully surprised to see the way I manage to get about. I was welcomed by all sorts & conditions of men, but the event was the reception by the Masai. There are 24 of them here being drilled as soldiers & they made an arrangement to meet me in the street. When they saw me coming they let out a yell & started a war dance. Then they made a rush, surrounded me & hugged me & kissed me & wept like a lot of children, & when I wanted to talk they said, "We can't talk today, we can only cry." Three of them had fits & there was great excitement all round.

A party of my old Kikuyu men has just come down, & I hear that all is well there & that Russell is very fit. Things here are pretty lively, what with the Regt. of Indians & all the Railway people, & the place has changed wonderfully for the better.

En route for Kikuyu. 6.7.96.

After sundry false starts here I am well on my way to Kikuyu. I had men & all ready to go to Mweli when I last wrote, but Martin asked Hardinge if he might go there as he is just married, & as Hardinge knew I was not keen on it, he allowed the exchange....I am travelling very slowly at first to get the men into trim, but hope to reach Kikuyu about 27th. Water is scarce for the next five days & requires a lot of arranging. I may have to do double marches....

....I had a very jolly time in Mombasa; of the sixteen nights I spent there, the Doctor & I only dined twice by ourselves. I dined out 13 times & once we had a party ourselves. When Hardinge left by the mail we had a great tumasha. At 9.30 a.m. a great durbar at which the various nationalities presented addresses; at 11 a.m. a great Champagne Lunch at the hospital given by us officers of the Protectorate. At 4 p.m. another great durbar for Craufurd, our Sub. Commr. at Mombasa, & in the evening there was a Nautch dinner given by the Indians to which we were all invited & had to go, a pretty gay day for Mombasa....

....I have had no fever as yet, though for two or three days in Mombasa I was very seedy & had to pile in quinine & am still taking it daily. Several fellows were down with slight bouts after the heavy rains but nothing serious. MacDonald[3] was in fine feather; during the 12 months not a single death had occurred in the hospital, though he had all the wounded men there, during the fighting besides his other patients; it speaks well for the place.

Whitehouse, the Chief Engineer of the Railway is a very good chap & his wife is also very nice. He went up the first 100 miles with Hardinge to Ndii & says it is the most awfully desolate country he has ever seen, though he has seen nearly every country in the world. The water & transport are worrying his life out. They are making a temporary wooden bridge from the island [Mombasa] to the mainland & have some of the earthworks ready this side. The advance survey is 30 miles inland now & they still hope to construct at the rate of 100 miles a year once they get on the mainland. They are increasing their staff every month & next month 3 engineers come out to go up to Kikuyu to tackle that part.

All our Sub. Commrs. have just been gazetted Vice-Consuls, so I have good news for John Ainsworth. I feel very proud of myself today, for I marched from camp to camp on foot, only about 10 or 11 miles, but it took 4 hours as the men are very out of condition & are heavily laden. One man carries my big leather trunk besides his blanket & 10 days food, so you may imagine he at least carries enough. With my Parsee friend in the transport office I arranged everything beautifully & had a few extra men to carry food for my horses. This of course gets used up & I can then ease off some of the other loads, but I have got the whole of my kit with me, except my dress clothes & white shirts which I left with a chum in Mombasa....

....I must now to bed for the drum goes at 4 a.m.

Kikuyu. July 31st. '96

At last I can head my letters from the old quarters. I arrived here on 25th. after a very fast trip from the coast, 23 days, & as I took 6 days over the first 45 miles, you may imagine I did not waste time over the last 300. Both my horses & my donkey are still very fit; if they live through the next fortnight I think I can reckon they are safe, which will be great luck.

On my arrival at Machakos I found Ainsworth had left for Kikuyu on a visit with Dr. Hinde[4] & Capt. Harrison;[5] the latter commands the forces of the Province, so I pushed on to catch them all here, sending an express ahead. Russell met me about five miles from the Fort & we strolled in. There was a huge concourse of natives, & what with the Masai dancing war dances & the mob all yelling & shouting, there was a great tumasha. My arm was nearly wrung off before I got into the Fort, & as I had done 25 miles in a broiling sun, I was not sorry to get into the house & have some tea.

We had a great evening, no less than eight of us sitting down to dinner. Ainsworth has improved wonderfully under the tuition of the Doctor & Harrison, both ripping good chaps, & I think we shall get on well. We had a great talk over the affairs of the nation & our general ideas coincide well. In about a month's time we intend to make a grand tour of Kikuyu right up to Kenia [Mt. Kenya] & all round the country & interview all the Chiefs &c. The place has altered wonderfully since so many Europeans have been about. Anyone can roam around now all over the country without fear & I don't think the natives will ever again try any tricks with us....

....All my Masai are doing well & behaving themselves, & I think the bad feeling engendered by the massacre[6] is pretty well forgotten. In fact I find things here generally much better than I was led to expect at the coast. Discipline is pretty slack in the Fort & several such details require reformation, but this will soon come alright. Gilkison is better in an office than out of it. The garden is in first rate condition & I had a couple of strawberries the day I arrived. There are some Europeans about 1000 yds. from the Fort, building stores for two Mombasa firms & one man coffee planting about 3 miles from here. I have selected a site for my house about half a mile from the Fort, & Ainsworth is going to build a house for himself close by it, for though he is ordered to keep his headquarters at Machakos, he intends to visit here as often as he can & both Harrison & the Doctor want to come & live here. I think the Govt. will build me a house & probably allow a certain quantity of furniture so I intend to build a comfortable show.

Ainsworth is having a deal of trouble with his people & a lot of my Masai are away with him now to assist in a little expedition. All the natives round here are very peaceable now & I hope will remain so. They have good crops & have made lots of money working for various Europeans, so are very contented....

....My kitten arrived here all well & has already caught several rats, so will be a godsend to the place. My boy, dog, antelope, monkeys & all are flourishing, so I feel quite at home again & there are plenty of my old men left, though I miss many who were killed in Kedong.

Kikuyu. Aug. 12th '96

Kikuyu is very different now to what it was when I left. So many Europeans have been knocking around that the natives are quite tame & I can ride anywhere around alone, though I generally take a mounted orderly so as to keep both horses exercised. The horses are very fit & getting almost too lively, but that is better than losing them.

The Major writes very cheerfully from Naivasha. It seems funny now getting notes & letters from all parts almost daily. We have a fortnightly Provincial mail, the usual monthly coast mails up & down, besides special runners from Machakos & Naivasha & from various people around....

....Everything here is in a terrible state of dilapidation & I am hard at work trying to get the place in order, but as I have no carpenters or anything, I have to do a deal of superintendence. I average five or six cases in court a day & have at present over 20 men on sick list per diem, all of whom have to be attended. My clerk has gone & also my hospital orderly & my old Kikuyu interpreter, so I am badly handicapped with Russell seedy as well. However I am as fit as can be & as active as a flea, so I mustn't grumble.

Kikuyu. Sept. 10th. '96.

I must just scrawl a few lines to let you see I am all fit, but I have had a burst of work this month & to crown my bad luck had to dismiss my clerk, a Goanese, for dishonesty, so had all the work myself. Russell is back from Machakos all well again & is to take charge of Ngong Sub-Station & look after the Masai. Lane remains as my Assistant here for a time & an old chap named Dugmore[7] is to accompany Russell to Ngong, nominally to command troops, but as there are only 15 men to command, the place is a sinecure & simply meant to get rid of him. He is a good old chap but very cranky & too fond of writing to the papers, so they have shifted him up here on to me....

....Lane & I have had some real good Sundays out on horseback & enjoyed it. I am improving roads all round & bridging streams so that we can get about better. The Masai are getting more in hand but it is a tough job to keep the Wakikuyu & Masai from quarrelling....

....Transport arrangements have broken down utterly & I have to send 100 men to Mombasa today to fetch up supplies for this Station. We are infinitely worse off than when we were under the Company for supplies, & Ainsworth & his people are all starving owing to drought & are drawing their food from here. Things are generally in a bad state. Every available man is being used on the Railway & we can get none for transport from the coast. What will happen until we get the Railway I know not; however we can scrape along with a few groceries & tobacco.

Kikuyu. Oct. 8th. '96

Another mail going, & as usual I have been wrestling with the a/cs up to the last moment. Lane is supposed to keep them, but he jumbles them up in such confusion that this time I have failed utterly to unravel them. However it will give them something to do at the coast & perhaps make them hurry up & send me a clerk. We have regular Auditors now, both in Uganda & at Mombasa, & they are awfully particular. I heard from Jackson[8] that nearly all officers in Uganda, including of course the Major & himself, get their a/cs back regularly for correction. Jackson thinks he would be perfectly justified, with thatched roofs, in having a periodical fire to simplify matters, but I'm afraid Govt. might object.

I have had an awfully worrying fortnight of it. The people at the coast sent Martin to engage 1000 men at once & buy food for two months supply for them for Railway work at Kibwezi; but they forgot to send any trade goods wherewith to buy the grain from the natives. Ainsworth & I found ourselves in an awful fix. However we tackled the job between us & somehow or other raked up all sorts of things & got the food in. I supplied about 20 tons of grain, all purchased in small lots in 12 days, & he got something less, for his District is terribly dried up....Now I have to supply 33,000 lbs. of grain monthly & a relief of 400 men every two months, so have plenty to do; and as all men they can get are being employed on the Railway, we can obtain no supplies from the coast & are in a hat. I suppose it will come out somehow, but it is a bit of a worry.

Martin & his wife came up & stayed here about 12 days. I gave them my quarters & we have had a very jolly time. She is Portuguese but very nice; she plays, & sings in several languages, & as old Dugmore has the American organ up here (that I brought out for him), we had some musical evenings. Russell on first whistle, Lane on banjo & Mrs. M. [Martin] on the organ, while I occasionally had to warble as my share, & another fellow named Trefusis plays the autoharp very well.

By the bye I shall be mentioning names you don't know, so must tell you that two Mombasa firms have agents up here living about 1000 yds. from the Fort.[9] Trefusis is a very good sort who has travelled the world, & a man named Walsh with his wife.[10] Then we have one coffee planter, Kitchen, & Dr. Wallace's party just coming. Mr Wallace (brother) & his wife[11] arrived about 10 days ago & Dr. Boedeker & wife,[12] & a Mr. McQueen & wife[13] are to arrive tomorrow. We shall then have 10 Europeans resident in Kikuyu & Dr. W. & his wife[14] later; they are delayed at the coast just now with Mrs. W. ill.

Did I tell you Edward Russell came back from Machakos very fit & is now in charge at Ngong, a Sub-Station under this one. They also sent me a detachment of Nubians, but I sent them off to Ngong where they can't get into mischief. Capt. Dugmore is in charge of them, so lives there with Russell, & Lane is here with me.

We had a grand parade of the outgoing & relieving forces, & after I had had a great pow-wow with all the Masai, Mrs. Martin, with my help, hoisted the flag; general salute, with three buglers each trying to outblow the other & all the bugles in different keys, & then three cheers for the Queen & the old garrison marched out with all proper formalities. The Masai enjoyed the fun, though I think they had an idea we were all mad. We christened the Fort Elvira after Mrs. Martin & together had a jolly day.

On Sunday, my birthday, I shall give a big dinner & invite all the newcomers. My cook is doing a month in chain-gang, but I think I must let him out a week earlier than he deserves, to cook the dinner. He is of course a Mission boy, an awful scoundrel, but a good cook....

....I have been writing hard for the best part of three days & nights, quarterly reports & goodness knows what & I'm about sick of it. If they don't send me a clerk shortly they get no more a/cs. I'll never dismiss another as long as I live unless I've got a man to put in his place.

Kikuyu. Nov. 4th '96

We had rare fun on my birthday. I gave a grand dinner & 14 Europeans sat down, including four married couples. A Dr. & Mrs. Boedeker. two of the settlers' party, are staying with me pro-tem; I cannot put them all up, & Mrs. B. superintended the table & cooking arrangements. We had a beautiful strip of silk down the table with flowers galore & everyone wore collars & neckties & generally looked respectable. Russell came in from Ngong & as we had old Dugmore's American organ here, we had a musical evening though it was Sunday. The settler's party consisted of Dr. B. & his wife; Wallace & his wife, farmer; McQueen & wife, blacksmith; & Dr. Wallace & wife. The last of these couples has not yet arrived as Mrs. Wallace was seedy at the coast. Besides these there are Walsh & his wife, both from South Africa; a man called Trefusis for Mackenzie's firm & a coffee planter called Kitchen....

....There was a bit of trouble with the Nubians at Ngong while they were here & R. [Russell] called me out about 8 o'clock at night. Fowler[15] came with me & I soon squared up the Nubians, & then he & I went out shooting but saw nothing. Ainsworth is a bit annoyed about the matter & is coming up next week to enquire into it. They have a Military Dept. here now & our relative duties appear to be somewhat of a mystery, so I expect a bit of a row. However R. was in the right & I shall back him up right through. Ainsworth has so far left me severely alone, & beyond worrying me with crowds of Officials which require answer, we get on alright. I am having an awful dose of office work, still being clerkless, but Lane takes a good deal of it. I have also an awful lot of District work, land disputes & worries between Masai & Wakikuyu. I have just settled a murder case which very nearly caused war between the two tribes....

....I have just heard that an engineer named Blackett, with two European assistants, is coming up to stay in Kikuyu to survey the line of rail through the District. He came out with Fowler & those other fellows & they say he is a splendid chap. Kikuyu will soon be the place of East Africa & I'm only afraid that later on they will appoint a Governor of East Africa stationed here & then I shall have to shift; but I hope that by that time I shall have got a step or two.

Kikuyu. Dec. 4th 1896

There has been very little doing here for the last month. The chief event was the arrival of a party of three to survey this District for the Uganda Railway. With them & Dr. & Mrs. Boedeker, my shanty is pretty full & we have great battles at four-handed crib or whist every night. Our Xmas party promises to be a big one, but unless our luxuries come up in time we shall have little to eat or drink. We cannot get loads up anyway; all the porters are employed on the Railway & even groceries nowadays have to be economized. I have been very hard at work trying to get all my work up to date, as I hope to get away in a few days to visit my District, taking a tour right up to Kenia. Harrison intends to join me & now it only remains to be seen if Lane is fit to take charge during my absence. This bout of his is a serious nuisance....

....The first European child was born in Kikuyu on 1st. December, Mrs. Wallace of a son.

Notes

1. Edward Hall, Francis Hall's elder brother, b 1851, d 1928.

2. Mwele, an Arab stronghold to the north of Mombasa and 15 miles inland. It was a focal point of an Arab rebellion in 1895-96 against the British anti-slavery policy. It ended when the 24th Baluchistan Regiment drove 3,000 rebels into German East Africa.

3. Walter Halliburton MacDonald LRCP, LRCS (Edin). Principal Medical Officer, East Africa Protectorate.

4. Dr. Sidney Langford Hinde, medical officer. Later a member of the Mackinder expedition to Mt. Kenya in 1899.

5. Captain Edgar Garston Harrison, (later Lieut. Col. Harrison CB DSO). Commissioned in the Duke of Wellington's regiment in 1885, he served in Ireland and India and was seconded to the King's African Rifles in 1895. Imported the first foxhounds to East Africa in 1900 and was known as "Pygmy" throughout his career.

6. The Kedong massacre, see pages following Chapter 4.

7. Captain F.S. Dugmore, administrative officer and Commander of Ngong Fort.

8. Frederick John Jackson, (later Sir Frederick), led an IBEA expedition to the Uganda border in 1889 to make treaties with various tribes, to mark out or establish stations on the way, and to search for Emin Pasha (Eduard Schnitzer) a German who was Governor of the Equatorial Province of the Sudan. Jackson was an official in the Uganda Administration 1894-01 and later became Governor of Uganda. Author of Birds of Kenya Colony and Uganda Protectorate.

9. The two firms were Smith, Mackenzie and Boustead & Ridley.

10. Known as Pioneer Mary to Europeans, Mary Walsh was reputed to have been the first female pioneer in Rhodesia and was certainly one of the earliest in British East Africa. Aged seventeen, she left Ireland with her first husband for the Australian outback. Twelve years later, following the deaths of her husband and two children (one child died from a snake bite, the other drowned), she travelled to Rhodesia where she met and married John Walsh. They trekked north to British East Africa and lived a semi nomadic life. She ran dairies, opened bars, tea-rooms and bakeries and travelled up and down the country with her transport business trading anything from combs to cooked chickens. The Africans called her Bibi Kiboko (Mrs. Rhinoceros) on account of the rhino-hide sjambok whip which she always carried and never hesitated to use if crossed. She wore men's puttees and carried a pearl-handled revolver in her skirts. She lost another seven children to malaria and sometimes went on wild, drunken binges when she would ride her mule backwards to amuse onlookers.

    John Walsh was a less flamboyant character and traded cattle and goats between Kikuyu, Machakos and Kibwezi.

11. W.T.E. Wallace and his wife Mary who was seven months pregnant when she arrived at

Fort Smith after a 375 mile march. They settled in Kikuyu District and became successful farmers.

12. Dr. Henry Albert Boedeker was Eurasian by birth and Parsee by religion, small in stature and dark skinned. He met his future wife Helen, the daughter of Sir Henry Wardlow of Tillicoutry, while studying medicine at Glasgow University. Their relationship and subsequent marriage was considered scandalous at the time and, in search of a new life together, they sailed for East Africa in June 1896 aboard the s.s. Goorka. Dr. Boedeker later became Nairobi's first Medical Officer.

13. James McQueen, a blacksmith from Dumfriesshire, and his wife Mary, a strong, six feet tall, practical Scotswoman who was two months pregnant at the end of her safari to Fort Smith. Following a journey to Uganda, the McQueens settled in Mbagathi, near Ngong. They hacked a farm, Rhino Farm, out of dense forest and built their homestead from available materials.

14. Dr. David Wallace was the brother of W.T.E. Wallace. His wife fell sick in Mombasa and they abandoned the idea of settling up-country and returned home.

15. Charles W. Fowler, Administrative officer.

Chapter 7

QUEEN VICTORIA'S JUBILEE

Kikuyu. Jany. 11th. '97.

Since last writing I have been fairly on the move & had a good tour right round Kikuyu, a thing I have been longing to do for years. Harrison, who is a keen sportsman, said that he thought I ought not to go without an escort & of course he would have to take charge of it. So we started together on 8th December & commenced by going out on the plains over a piece of ground that has hitherto never been explored. I fairly excelled at map making & sent in quite a swagger map of our route.

We saw any amount of ordinary game the first day & no less than 12 rhino, but we wanted buffalo so didn't shoot anything else. At last we came on an old solitary buffalo & filled him up with lead but he still went, & as it was heavy jungle we had to proceed cautiously. I was leading on my big horse & Harrison close behind when two lions charged us. H. jumped off but said he couldn't see over the jungle, & as the lions stood about 15 paces off & hesitated, we circled off back into the open & then bombarded them. We wounded both, but they hid in the jungle & we spent an exciting two hours looking for them, but though one snarled within 10 ft. of us, we did not get him for he slunk away. The fact was we were a bit over-cautious & gave them time, but perhaps it was just as well, for two wounded lions &

a wounded buffalo are rather too many to walk up to at one time. So we consoled ourselves with the thought that though we had no game, at all events we hadn't a funeral to attend.

The following day we saw 9 lions strolling about, but bagged none, & rhino were a perfect nuisance on the path. We had to bridge a river & swim our horses & cows over, but it was soon done, for I had a lot of my old hands & they all knew their work. Our horses became quite used to swimming, for we had to swim them about 5 times during the trip, but the cows objected & declined to give us any milk after they had swum a river.

We struck almost due East from the Fort, then North up to the Sagana (Tana) river near Kenia, then back through all the inhabited part of Kikuyu towards Naivasha, up to Kinangop & then home. We were away 15 days & only rested one day, so covered some ground. The natives, though very timid in some places, received us very well everywhere, & once they knew who I was, brought in presents & treated us royally. For the first five days we were in the wilds & saw no one; but then we passed through one inhabited District for two days, & again into the hills by the Sagana river. We wanted to cross this into Meranga [Muranga] District, just at the foot of Kenia, but the river was in flood & about 100 yds. broad. We could only have crossed by a raft but had no time to spare as we both wished to be back for Xmas, so turned back.

From the Sagana right up to Kinangop we travelled along the top of a high ridge with big valleys on each side. The country is simply lovely, densely populated & every inch cultivated; miles upon miles of bananas & yams. The vines of the latter they train on standards, & as they are all in lines, they look exactly like hops. From every little gully there was a waterfall & splendid rushing rivers in the bottom of every valley. It was all very nice for these two days, but when we had to turn South & cut across the valleys, we didn't appreciate the scenery quite so much. We travelled one day of hard marching for 8 hours & slept within sight of, & only 6 miles distant from, our previous camp. I never saw such a rugged country in my life. It was like a giant ploughed field; each furrow a V-shaped gully about 500 ft. deep & you had no sooner got out of one than you were into another. Many were so steep that we couldn't ride & I had to clamber up one hill for 35 mins. on my hands & feet, the only way to tackle it. Though I had picked porters, they could not stand it & said they would rather go to the Ravine & face the cold 50 times over than travel this road again. We shall certainly never attempt to cross it again, but shall go round, & down the spurs of hills when we want to get to a place.

We discovered some beautiful waterfalls; in many places a large river going over an 80 or 100 ft. fall, a grand sight, & we crossed one river about 25 miles from here on a beautiful bridge of solid rock. The rock on top was about 40 ft. above water, about 10 ft. broad, & is well used by the natives. Underneath, the rock is fully 20 ft. clear of the water, the whole covered with creepers & bush on the sides, & the road nice & clear.

We crossed over another river by a native foot-bridge most artfully made. Advantage had been taken of two trees, one of which overhung the river. An approach was built to the boughs of one & poles laid to the second. The poles were slung by a network of fibre ropes from the upper boughs of this to the upper bough of one on the opposite side, thus forming a suspension bridge over the main span with net-work on both sides. I tried to draw it but seem to have made a mess of it. However it will give you some notion that the natives in those parts have fairly advanced ideas.

Of course we were close under Kenia, so saw some grand views of it, & although we were within 30 miles of the peaks, they were always in clouds in the heat of the day, but we managed to fix our camps by them most days. We were considerably over 8000 ft. towards Kinangop, amongst bracken, blackberries, ferns of all kinds, forget-me-nots, wild violets & all sorts of European plants, & as for temperature I found four blankets none too many in a closed tent, & one morning there was a heavy white frost on the ground. We carried tents, & blankets for our horses, & they not only did well, but actually grew fat on the journey with the steady exercise & plenty of grain.

We arrived back at the Fort on 23rd. Dec. so I had very little time to arrange anything for Xmas. But I thought we ought to have some fun, so I arranged Athletic Sports for the men in the morning, a shooting match for the Europeans in the afternoon & a big dinner in the evening & we carried it through nobly.

The Sports were great fun & over 200 natives of all sorts & sizes started for the 1000 yds. race straight along the road. I was starter & formed them all up in two lines across & then loosed them off, & after sundry false starts they all tried to get on to a 20 ft. road at once, & a flock of sheep at a narrow gate was nothing to it. I rode behind & whipped in & the excitement was great amongst the crowd. We had an extraordinary collection of natives here, as there was a caravan of Waganda & Wasoga[1] camped here, so we had a team from each tribe for the tug of war; no less than seven teams going in for it, & the Soudanese eventually won. The Wakikuyu made a splendid fight of it with the Wasoga, pulling for over 4 mins. & there was frightful enthusiasm when the Wakikuyu won. We finished the 8 events by about 1.30 p.m. & then all had lunch, & us Europeans had a shooting match afterwards. The shooting all round was very bad, especially at the longer range, & I was third out of the 11 or 12 shooting.

In the evening we had a big dinner party; 15 sat down & we enjoyed ourselves thoroughly. Of course, my loads of luxuries never arrived, though they were ordered 3 months ago, so we had to do our best with what we could muster & had a really first rate feed & just enough whiskey to drink to absent friends. Supplies had run so low that we couldn't do another dinner for New Year, but the neighbours all came in after dinner & we had Auld Lang Syne round the table at midnight.

The time since then has been anything but pleasure; trying to get the year's a/cs right & we are still hard at it. I took three days off, having to go away to settle a land dispute amongst some natives, & only returned last night. The Railway Engineers went with me to look at the country & we had a very jolly trip, living on wild ducks the whole time. We were 7,800 ft. above the sea so it was bitterly cold. Blackett, the Chief Engineer, says tropical Africa is a fraud he has only light clothing so feels the cold....

....We are at present completely cut off from the coast & can get no supplies up, loads ordered six months ago not having arrived yet. What it will be like until the Railway gets up I don't know. What is worse, we are down to native tobacco to smoke which is pretty awful. Lane received 1 lb. of baccy up by post & they charged him 6 Rupees postage from Mombasa, so it cost 10/= per lb. here & I took half to go on with. We shall soon have to evacuate our Stations unless arrangements are made to supply us, or give up groceries & tobacco & live a la Kikuyu....

....By the bye, little Ted[2] should keep all our Protectorate stamps; the name is already changed to East African Protectorate, leaving out the "British," so those stamps with "British" on them may become rare....

....I was terribly shocked to hear of poor Eusty's death. Little did I think, when I said goodbye to him at Charing X, it was the last time I should see him. I thought of writing to Uncle John & to Alice, but my letters would arrive so long after, that I think it better left alone....Eusty & I were always great friends & there are two or three of the old Company's men out here who will be very sorry to hear the news. I couldn't believe it at first, it seemed so improbable. Life is as uncertain in London as in Africa.

I hope you have got over the effects of your fall. You must be careful Dad, for at your age falling out of apple trees is not exactly healthy exercise....

....I forgot to tell you, & also to tell Bee, that the baby was christened Francis George Kikuyu Wallace & I was God-father, but as I had to be out at Ngong, Lane was my proxy & I got out of a long service. I was also away on Sunday so haven't graced one of their services yet. I expect you will hear from the Vicar something of the Missionaries' ideas of Kikuyu & all of us. They are very friendly & gushing to us but may report home very differently.

Kikuyu. Jany. 28th '97.

The Missionary caravan left here on 16th & the ladies sent in a very effusive letter to me thanking me for the kindness & hospitality they had received during their lengthy stay here. Tell Georgie[3] if she wants to send me a present to get the "Church Missionary Gleaner" with the account of Kikuyu & then send it. I am very anxious to see what they say. Russell had a sore foot & asked the Missionary doctor to look at it, & after they had left, R. sent him a present of a fat sheep. In a letter in reply, he begs Russell "to accept definitely the gift of everlasting life" in return. R. thinks he has done rather a good trade at that rate. Can you imagine any sane man writing such utter rot?....

....I gave Lane a bit of an outing to go & punish an Mkikuyu Chief who had been doing a little murdering on his own account & refused to come in. Our force was joined by all the natives for miles around & Lane says that when he arrived on the ground, about 25 miles from here, he had a following of about 4000. So our friend made himself scarce & left Lane to collect his goats & cattle without opposition. Lane picnicked there for a week & enjoyed it. On the way home the friendlies helped themselves pretty freely to goats day & night, for of course Lane had to get them to herd; however he came back with 240 head of cattle & 2000 goats, a pretty good haul. A few more like this & Kikuyu will pay for itself.

The most terrible news we have heard is that the whole of Kenia District, including all these parts, is to be reserved for game, the regulations strictly enforced & apply to all Govt. officials as well as others. This is very hard lines & puts an end to all our shooting unless we apply for leave & go outside the District. I'm off in a few days to do all I can before the actual orders arrive.

The Railway people have already surveyed from the plains up past here, a steady grade of 1 in 50 which is not out of the way. They are at present camped close by & Blackett is going with me for a trip down Athi way on Monday....

....A German gentleman named Schillings has just passed down from Uganda, the rest of his party, a German scientific expedition, coming on behind. We had orders from the Foreign Office about these people months ago so have to look after them well. He shot three lions on the plains the day after leaving here & wrote me a note to say how pleased he was.

One of the events of the month was the birth of a little antelope, the offspring of Billy & Nanny, my two tame ones; the first case of them breeding in captivity.

I told you in my last that we are now in the Postal Union, so the Post-Master's job is added to my multifarious duties & soon I shall be head gamekeeper too I suppose. I shall want a large stud of horses to get through half my work. As it is, my two get plenty of work running out to Ngong & spinning out of an evening, but they want it for they are fat enough for anything.

Kikuyu. March 23rd. '97.

You will have been wondering why you didn't get a letter from me last mail. I was properly sold; the Major came in & dragged me off hurriedly to go to Naivasha to settle some troubles with the natives there. He has to rely on the natives of my District for food, & as they boycotted him, he was in a fix. I reckoned to be back in plenty of time for the mail but the coast people altered the date, making it four days earlier, so I missed it altogether. I enjoyed my trip most thoroughly. The last time I was up there was when I tackled the leopard & was carried back....

....While at Naivasha, Whitehouse, the Chief Engineer of the Railway, came up on a camel with Blackett, our Dist. Engineer. The sudden change of climate tried Whitehouse, for he came up in 21 days from the intense heat of Mombasa, & he had a bad bout of fever on the road. Blackett & I had a day's shooting in Kedong Valley....Tomorrow he & I go off up to the top of the mountains to try to find a way down for the Railway. I know a line I think will prove feasible; if so it will save no end of expense in building. When he left, Whitehouse had nearly all his Europeans & 50% of his Indians in hospital with fever. It has been a very bad season down there; first extraordinary rains & then intense heat, the natural consequence being any amount of fever & one or two cases of sunstroke. The rail-head is now 30 miles from Mombasa

& they hope to reach Kibwezi, 200 miles, by March next. So when I bring Bee out, we shall be able to do most of the journey by Railway, which will save vast trouble & expense....

....While I was at Naivasha my Somalis returned from Berbera bringing two ponies for me. The one was very ill when it arrived, & in spite of all that we could do, it died a week or so later. The other is a very good serviceable beast so I am keeping him & have got rid of Sultan the big grey. He was a bit too big for me with my stiff leg. I had to be lifted onto him which was awkward, & as I had a fair offer from Harrison, we parted. I have not done so badly. My four horses cost me 1000 Rupees & I sold Sultan for 700. I have two good useful ponies left for 300 Rupees & I could sell either or both @ 500 apiece any day, so I can't lose much. I also had a piece of bad luck with a puppy that Jenner[4] sent me, half bloodhound, half foxhound, a grand beast, but like the pony it only arrived here to die. It is evidently a bad season to bring anything up from the coast.

I went down to Machakos to stay for a few days to talk over things generally with Ainsworth. I put up with Harrison but we all messed together in Ainsworth's house. A Mission Station in his District has just burst up for want of funds, so John has three ladies staying in the house one of whom I think will probably become the future Mrs. John.

Kikuyu. April 20th '97

Here we are at Easter Tuesday & the year going on apace. The weather too is keeping up its reputation, for we are sitting with a roaring fire & it is a steady cold drizzly rain outside that looks pretty miserable & makes the fire very cheerful.

I have had the roof of my house raised a couple of feet which makes the rooms far more airy and comfortable, & as the verandah now has more pitch, it doesn't leak like it used to. As for work I don't know which way to turn, there is so much to do....

....I was roused this morning by sad news. My pet Thomsonii, "Billy," the big old paterfamilias, broke his leg somehow in the night. I have put it into splints but I'm afraid that he is too restless a character for it ever to get well. He has now been four years in the Fort so I shall be very sorry to lose him....

....Blackett & I did a glorious trip for seven days. I took him a new line over the mountains. I got guides & arranged the whole thing & the result was we found a splendid route, much shorter than the old one & a better gradient off the escarpment down to Naivasha Lake. B. was so pleased that he moved the whole of his camp out at once to make a detailed survey of it. We travelled along a regular chain of small mountain tarns full of water-fowl. We had some grand duck shooting nearly every evening, & as we had no rain, thoroughly enjoyed the trip. Our meals consisted of a duck each three times a day, with soup, vegetables &c. in addition, yet we always seemed hungry, for it was pretty bracing at 7,800 ft., a lovely country with bracken, brambles & all kinds of ferns growing everywhere....

....We have been experiencing a very bad time with jiggers, the burrowing flea. The poor beggars of men with bare feet get full of them, & unless they take them out regularly, which means digging holes in the feet with a pointed stick, ulcers form & they get very bad. I have averaged 34 men per diem useless this last month out of 200. Europeans do not suffer too much, but one has to have one's feet examined frequently & the jigger removed. This plague has come all across Africa & the only consolation is that it passes off to a certain extent, especially in cold climates, so in time we may hope to get rid of them....

....I have just reaped my barley & oats before the rains; the latter is for seed & I hope now to be able to feed my horses if the next crop is as great a success. We have been very busy tree planting & are still at it. The quick growing blue-gum is the favourite, but I also have a few pines in & a note has just reached me from Watt, the Missionary who came here three years ago & is now near Machakos, that he has some nice young fig-trees & grape vines to sell, so I shall certainly order some....

....On Easter Sunday we amused ourselves by assisting the Doctor to amputate a man's leg in the morning, & in the afternoon invited the whole European population, including Francis George Kikuyu, to a tea-fight. Mrs. S. made a heap of jam tarts, cakes &c. and we all ate more than was good for us & enjoyed it thoroughly. Russell spent Saturday to Monday here but there was no Bank Holiday for us as it is mail time.

There are to be a few changes of Officers next month & several new ones are coming out, but I don't think there is any chance of my being shifted unless I get promotion, & it is possible that in time I may get my step without being shifted, for there is some idea of making Kikuyu & Masailand one Province under a Sub. Commr. for which post only the Major would rank ahead of me....

....The settlers are busy ploughing & the Doctor makes a good deal by odd fees. The blacksmith is a very handy man & a good farrier. He pares all the horses feet, mends baths, rifles or anything, so will get on.

Kikuyu. May 18th '97

We have had quite a festive week. Dr. Hinde & Moloney, Lt. R.A., who was mauled by a lion, came up, & Foaker, one of the old Coy's hands arrived with his wife en route for Uganda, so we had a jolly party. We finished up on Sunday by seeing them all off to the first camp about 5 miles out & having a picnic. I took the bullock cart to carry the ladies when they were tired & we had a very jolly day, returning in the cart by moonlight.

The second birth took place in Kikuyu on Sunday, a Mrs. McQueen, the blacksmith's wife, being confined of a son, another little Kikuyu. F.G. Kikuyu is doing splendidly & I only hope this one will follow his example. I think the climate is quite good enough for children....

....Russell gets his opportunity for he is appointed "Acting Dist. Officer" & should not be long in having it confirmed. Gilkison, who acted for me, has been taken off District work & made Transport & Storekeeper at the coast. MacQuarrie I hear is attached to Railway work, so there are only two District Officers left, MacDougall at Melindi & myself, & four Sub. Commrs., Craufurd, Rogers, Jenner & Ainsworth. So by the time they get the staff up to proper strength I shall be well towards the head of the list. The Consul Genl. has been expected up here for months but I think he is too busy with the slave matters on the coast to be able to get away.

I have just received a most terrible "Official" asking for particulars of the population of Kikuyu, "proportionate number of free men & slaves &c." In fact if they sent an expedition of Royal Engineers they couldn't answer all the questions. Fortunately they say they are fully aware that such estimates must be, to a certain extent, "conjectural." You would never believe the number of Regulations we get up here. The latest was very amusing. a "Regulation for the protection of the property of women." This in a country where women never possess anything is too ridiculous. However they make my notice board look very imposing & I shall soon be able to paper the house.

Kikuyu. June 14th 1897

I have been enjoying very busy times, & to crown everything the cattle plague has broken out among the Masai cattle & they have smallpox at Machakos, so we are likely to have a repetition of our experiences of '92.

However I have investigated the cattle business thoroughly & found it to be pleuro-pneumonia, what they call "lungsigte" in the South. For this there is only one preventative & that is inoculation, like vaccination. I spent 3 or 4 days with the Masai & explained the whole thing to them, & for natives I have never seen any take such a keen & intelligent interest in such a matter. They allowed me to slaughter one of the sick beasts & on seeing that the lungs were in exactly the state I had described, they were quite satisfied that I was Ngai (God). They brought me 30 beasts to be inoculated & said if they saw it was effectual I was to come & operate on all their cattle. They said it was very simple but could only be effectual if done by me as "my hands were good," a truly Oriental way of shirking work & paying a compliment at the same time. But I have not the slightest doubt that if the disease spreads they will send for me, & by inoculating, & thereby saving the greater part of their cattle, I shall do more to settle the Masai question than could be done by a big war. One piece of history I learned was that it was this disease which killed off all the buffalo, cattle & bovine antelope seven years ago, a fact which has hitherto been disputed....

....We are busy preparing for Jubilee Day. Lane is going to Machakos where they are going to have horse races, the "Diamond Jubilee Cup" & the Machakos Cup. Lane is going to take one or possibly both of my ponies & his own, so we hope to bring back at least one cup to Kikuyu. We were out for a gallop this morning, but my pony was heavily handicapped as I was riding 2 stones heavier than Lane & the Somali. Here we are going to have Athletic Sports in the morning for the natives, at noon a feu de joie & march past & a grand gorge of beef for all hands. I have 12 bullocks to kill. The Europeans will all lunch here & at 3 p.m. we have a shooting match for Europeans & a grand dinner in the evening. I have a small keg of whiskey which the Major sent me & have been saving it up for the occasion, so shall be able to supply the wants of the thirsty, & having a rather good cook, hope to serve a decent dinner. I have invited all the natives, Masai & Wakikuyu, so we shall have a big gathering, & with about 17 Europeans shall beat Machakos in numbers. I hope you send me some of the illustrated papers after the Jubilee, for I should awfully like to see them. I would give anything to see the procession, but I am always in the wilds when these things occur.

Yours of 9th April reached me this mail, also 23rd April. You seem surprised to think that I shall be home next year early, but I hope if all goes well to get short leave of 4 months from Mombasa to run home & fetch Bee. I am entitled to four months after 20 months service which would be in February

'98, & if there are not too many men home on sick leave at the time, I hope to manage it....

....The garden & crops are a sight - I could supply all of Tonbridge with vegetables & then have plenty to spare. The natives too have had splendid crops so food is plentiful.

I have just heard that MacDonald, who surveyed the Railway, is coming up again "proceeding to the interior" but as he wants enormous supplies of food, livestock &c., I conclude he is on some Secret Mission towards the Nile.

Kikuyu. July 31st '97

And now for an account of our "Jubilee." I was left alone to engineer the whole thing as Lane went down to Machakos in charge of the "stud" to race for the Machakos Cup.

Our programme commenced at 9.30 a.m. with Athletic Sports. There were some 2000 to 3000 natives on the ground & the entries were very numerous & competition keen. The Masai won the long distance races easily; the sack & obstacle races created immense amusement & the only pity was that we hadn't time to run more heats of each. The Tug-of-War was splendid; teams of Wakikuyu pulling for nearly 5 minutes before the Masai won, & they then pulled against the troops, & after 3 splendid pulls the troops won amidst intense excitement. This finished the Sports sharp to time at 11.45 a.m.

Then the troops & all my police, some 80 all told, fell in at noon & we had a general salute, feu de joie & three cheers for the Queen & then a march past &c. After this the meat of 12 oxen killed in the morning was served out indiscriminately & a general holiday to all hands.

At 12.30 p.m. all the Europeans, together with the Goanese clerks & two native Officers sat down to a stupendous lunch, but just as we were about to sit down, someone reminded me that I had said the white men would pull the winners of the Tug-of-War. So out we sailed, fell in the troop team & started. We had one native Officer, which rather spoilt it, but no one cared to object on such an occasion. The soldiers beat us the first pull, then I arranged my men & we beat them the second. The excitement amongst all the people was quite exhilarating & we all layed down to the third determined to win or die, & the rope broke & we all flopped down like pancakes. This fairly astonished the natives, & of course they attributed it entirely to the wonderful power of the "Mzungu," i.e. white man. We soon tied up the rope & then had an awful pull which nearly finished us all, but we managed to get the best of it & won the bout. Then we returned triumphant to enjoy our lunch.

Mrs. Boedeker, who had promised to make me some cakes &c. for tea, only turned up just before lunch, & then we found that in addition to cakes &c. she had made the most excellent beef-steak pie, in a wash hand basin too, no toy thing, & we ate it by the cubic foot. The meat was tender, the jelly perfect & the crust light, & I don't know when I have enjoyed anything so much, & to prove our appreciation we ate the lot. A 4 gal. keg of whiskey, on tap, which the Major had sent me, was also greatly appreciated & the after effects of lunch were such that no one felt inclined to stir from their seat. However at 3.30 p.m. I insisted on the programme & we went to arrange our shooting match (Europeans). We were not in good form, needless to state. Some said it was the Tug-of-War, others honestly confessed it was the lunch, but whatever the cause, the shooting was not exactly good; but of the 9 who fired I managed to come out first, & besides winning the toy prize given by Mrs. Boedeker, won a case of whiskey on a private match between Blackett & myself, each shooting with strange rifles. The shooting finished at sundown & we rested until 7.30 p.m. when all assembled here for dinner. The ladies had decorated the room & table & it never looked better, & my cook fairly excelled himself even though he had sampled the whiskey-keg pretty freely while we were shooting. Everything went without a hitch & we put the tables on one side & danced & had plantation walks round the grounds to the music of the harmonium, violin, accordion (played by my cook, Missionary native) & the flute until the small hours, when we had the usual National Anthem & Auld Lang Syne, & I for one got to bed just done to a turn after my day's work.

Next day we were all very cheap & limp when in came a runner with a note from Lane to say that my pony "Tempest" had won the Machakos Cup & Lane's mare 2nd. This livened us up & we celebrated another Jubilee & my visitors carried a resolution unanimously that none should leave until the keg of whiskey was finished in honour of the event, & they kept it too. I was awfully pleased about the Cup, for the competition between Machakos & Kikuyu was awfully keen, & though my Somalis declared "Tempest" would win, I never expected it for a moment. It was certainly a lucky day for me. My team won the Tug-of-War in which of course I pulled myself; then I won the shooting match, the Machakos Cup with Tempest, & the next day my boy came rushing in to say that my dog "Romp" had whipped

"Shetani," the champion dog & he said, "Why bwana, you beat all the white men yesterday & now Romp beats all the dogs." We certainly had a great "Jubilee;" everyone went in to enjoy themselves with a will & did it royally, & thanks to the hearty good will of everybody the day went off without a hitch & Europeans, natives & all were delighted & are never likely to forget it....
....Shortly after this came the first news from the coast of MacDonald's expedition, which worried us a bit, & then one day I received a letter from Major Ternan from Uganda saying that they were ordered to provide 1000 loads of food & couldn't do it, so that I must do my best to supply it. This nearly gave me a fit. So I saddled up my pony "Punch" & rushed down to Machakos, 47 miles in the day, & talked the matter over with Ainsworth. The next day I came half way back & they sent a tent & blankets out for me & I arrived on the third morning. Since then we have been hard at it....In 16 days I bought nearly 50 tons of native flour & had it bagged & stacked, besides making the bags. Not a soul on the Station had any rest, but now thank goodness, that is done & my present worry is to get enough natives to carry it. It is the biggest job we have ever had to do yet in this line but I think we shall get through with it, & once MacDonald has passed, I shall give the garrison a week's holiday to make up for it, for they are working like bricks & very cheerfully too.

Kikuyu. Aug. 15th '97.

The latest sensation here was the arrival some ten days ago of a camel caravan which had come right through from Berbera. The owner & leader was young Cavendish, nephew of the Duke of Devonshire, & his chum, a fellow named Andrew, a Lieut. of the 42nd. They had made a splendid trip round Lake Rudolph, an unexplored part, & had some grand sport. They were both awfully good fellows & stayed a week here with us during which we had a real good time....Cavendish is quite a boy, but has travelled a good deal & has any amount of money. He intends to return here next year, so has lent me his double 10 bore rifle until he returns, so there is no fear of me not having heavy enough metal now for rhino &c. It is about as heavy as I care to fire & is a splendid gun which costs about £50, so I was in luck, but as it weighs about 14 lbs. & fires 8 drams of powder, it is no toy & takes an extra man to carry it. I expect you will hear of Cavendish & Andrew when they get home, for they have discovered a new lake, two volcanoes (active) & probably one or two new species of antelope &c., not bad work for one trip....

....Did I tell you that I got a beautiful lot of young fruit trees up some time ago; four kinds of figs, 3 of grapes, & oranges, lemon & limes. So in a year or so we ought to have plenty of fruit & they are all doing well. My potatoes are something too grand this season. Nothing could beat them for size or flavour & they are the envy & admiration of all passers by. The camel brigade took down a load to Zanzibar just to show the people there what we can do.

Kikuyu. Oct. 31st. 1897.

It seems ages since I last wrote for I was away when the last mail was due to leave & only had 24 hours in which to get through all the official work for the end of the quarter. I was ordered out to a place about 25 miles from here to investigate some native troubles & couldn't get through the job in time to get back & write any mail in peace. We have had rather a heavy time lately, what with the visits from the Auditor & Sundry Others, Commandant of troops &c. & now the "Commissioner & Consul General" is close by so we are getting things in spick & span order for him. Having Lane here & two clerks I get away for District work more often, & as this is preferable to office work I don't lose any chances of getting out. The Auditor is a very nice fellow & I am glad to say didn't find my stock in a very bad state. I was some cloth & beads short, but not nearly so much as other Stations, & it is impossible to keep exactly right when you are paying out strings of beads & yards of cloth in large quantities....

....Now I hear Hardinge is at Machakos with Dr. MacDonald the P.O.M., my old friend of Mombasa Hospital, & Kestell-Cornish, one of the Consuls from Zanzibar. I could not understand why the last was coming, but Ainsworth informed me the other day that he intended to get married at once to a Miss Scott[5] who lives at Machakos, so I presume Cornish is up in his official capacity as marriage officer & the event will come off at once. I can't say that any of the rest of us think much of Miss Scott. She is plain, very quiet, Scotch-American with a twang & not at all good style. However she has played her cards well & perhaps they will suit each other. John A. was very affable when he came here & seemed very pleased about everything.

After his visit I got away with Blackett & Welby of the Survey party for a few days shooting & we explored Suswa, an extinct volcano about 25 miles from here....It was the sort of mountaineering I like, for we rode on horseback from the foot of the mountain to the edge of the crater comfortably. The main crater is about 5 & a half miles in diameter but is mostly a fairly level plain covered with game & here we camped. Then there is a second crater inside which is a most wonderful place. From where we stood, the edge was about 500 ft. sheer down; the bottom the most fearful chaos of lava & huge crevasses. A sort of huge moat was surrounding a mountain which rose about 1000 ft. sheer out of the centre, the diameter of this inside crater being about 1 & a half miles. It was a most wonderful sight & made one's hair stand on end to see some of our men on the very edge rolling boulders down. We found two steam vents, showing the thing is not quite extinct. The heat was tremendous out of these holes & one couldn't stand near in the full blast. I think we are the first Europeans who have ascended this mountain but I shall certainly make a show place of it now that I know the way up & how easy it is....

....It has been decided to make the Railway over the new route that I showed them & not go MacDonald's route. I am very pleased as it will open up a good deal more of the District & goes through a prettier bit of country. The rail-road is now about 120 miles from the coast, but a good deal of it is construction line & none too good at that from all I can hear....

....We are particularly lucky in the [Railway] party we have here. We all get on splendidly together which, I believe, is not the usual thing down towards the coast. One engineer has been sent away owing to his inability to get on with either Europeans or natives. Russell now has the Railway past his door at Ndii, so is revelling in such luxuries as bottled beer &c. from the coast.

We have no further news from Uganda or up the road, & the mails have not arrived, so I'm inclined to think things are not quite peaceful. This mutiny & desertion of 300 troops who were to have escorted MacDonald's party is a somewhat serious thing & I hear that at both Naivasha & the Ravine Stations they have taken away all the ammunition from the Nubian troops,[6] so their garrisons are not much value to them....

....Our safety here lies in having the Masai to play off against the Wakikuyu & vice versa. Either would fight the other with the greatest gusto if ordered to do so & there is not the slightest fear of them ever combining. So of course my work is to keep the peace & play them off on each other when necessity arises.

Kikuyu. Dec. 20th 1897

The Consul-Genl., Sir Arthur Hardinge, came to pay an official visit for the first time, accompanied by Dr. MacDonald, my old friend of Mombasa, & Kestell-Cornish, one of the Vice-Consuls, & of course Ainsworth. We had already heard of the mutiny of the Nubians but did not think much of it. However the day after they arrived I had a letter from Wilson, who is in Command at Naivasha, asking me to come at once & help him, as he was afraid his garrison intended to mutiny & he was in fear of his life, on watch day & night with the lock of the Maxim in his pocket. This was not cheerful news, but as I couldn't spare enough men to start off at once, the C.G. sent for-Harrison & the troops from Machakos & decided we would all go together. In the meantime I took them out to Ngong, introduced Lenana, the Chief of the Masai, & they went on to his village while I returned to arrange for transport &c. as I was to be Transport Officer for the column.

Lane took the order to Machakos on horseback in record time & Harrison started & marched his 100 men through the 47 miles in two days. I had everything ready here & we left on 10th Nov. for Naivasha.

We did record marching & reached there early on the 3rd day & promptly took possession of the Fort. I was for disarming the Nubians at once, but the C.G. addressed them in Arabic & told them they would have to go to Machakos at once & stay there until all the troubles were over, so out they went.

From Naivasha we pushed on by forced marches to the Ravine & arrived there early on the 8th day from Kikuyu, 130 miles. Of the 415 men we started with, one was left behind as he had run a thorn into his foot & had to stay at Naivasha. The C.G. was again averse to disarming the men, so we played the same game as at Naivasha; that is we stood in front of all the garrison while the C.G. harangued them in Arabic, which by the bye, being pure Egyptian Arabic, was Greek to all those who have never been North of Khartoum, & gave them a beautiful opportunity of cleaning us all off the face of the earth. However we had our own troops handy & the Maxim cleared for action, which was slightly better than at Naivasha....

....I can't tell you how delighted Martin & Wilson were to see us, for they had been living in abject fear of their lives for days. All the Stations between the Ravine & Mumias had been vacated, so we could do nothing more, & after giving the men a couple of days rest, we started back at the same wild pace that we went up.

On our return here I had to sit down & make out schemes & estimates for the transport of an Indian Regiment from the coast to Uganda. I started by saying it was impossible with our present resources & then propounded various schemes, which of course they will never attempt to carry out, but that is not my fault....

....On 15th the first detachment of India troops, 150 Sepoys from the Indian contingent at Mombasa, arrived under Scott, an old chum. They had previously written to say all their transport was arranged, but three days before they arrived, he wrote himself to say that it was only arranged as far as Kikuyu & I was to make further arrangements. This is the usual way they work at the coast. They think Kikuyu is William Whiteleys[7] & all they have to do is to send people up. However there were some Cape wagons here, so I seized them & a few carts. Most of the oxen were untrained but that was a detail. Unfortunately for me, in a weak moment, qualms of conscience made me promise Scott that I would help him with the wagons for the first few miles, & this start fairly eclipsed anything I had ever dreamt of, much less experienced.

We started with 20 oxen in each wagon, thinking a few extra would make things easier, but it only made confusion worse confounded, for each ox made up its mind to do as it pleased. Some turned somersaults, some preferred lying down, some turned round to see what was behind them & some thought they could go much better alone, so broke loose & went. After hours of this sort of game we were getting somewhat weary & the chances of reaching Uganda before the Railway seemed remote....In the afternoon the main body moved on & we made a valiant attempt at a fresh start with 50 Sepoys at each wagon. We got the first wagon up the hill & it actually progressed about half a mile; then a Sepoy managed to get his rifle in the wheel & fell with the rifle across his ankle. The wheel went over the butt & smashed his ankle badly. In the meantime we had all gone back to the second wagon which defied all our efforts to move it, & on hearing of the accident in front, Scott took my pony to go on to see the man, leaving me in charge of the wagon.

I tried every dodge I knew to make those oxen pull, & eventually, dead beat, we outspanned at 9 in the evening, made fires & bivouacked. At midnight the Doctor who was with the column returned with my pony & we then adjourned to a camp a little way off where we had a cup of tea & some biscuits & cold meat & shook down on some boxes for a few hours rest. At 4 in the morning I tackled the wagon again & was just giving up when some empty wagons arrived from Uganda way & relieved ours of some of the loads & after that I left, having had the toughest day's manual labour I have had for years.

Kikuyu. Feby. 28th 1898

It seems ages since I last wrote, but I have been nearly worried out of my wits these last two months arranging transport, supplies &c. for the troops going up to Uganda. I had been hoping to be well on my way home long before this, but they keep me here hanging on waiting for my relief & no one seems able to tell me when he will arrive....

....I am sending down a cablegram by this post to let you know my leave is postponed. I hope you get it & let Bee know. It is an awful nuisance. However I shall be home at a better time of year & Berkeley tells me they are sure to give me a couple of months extension of leave. I hope Bee won't be worried at the delay, it can't be helped.

Notes

1. Ugandan tribes.
2. Francis Hall's nephew, his elder brother Ted's son.
3. Georgina, Francis Hall's sister.
4. A.C.W. Jenner, Sub-Commissioner at Kismayu. Famous for his recommendation that every British official arriving in East Africa should be given several medals immediately and that one medal should be removed for every punitive expedition in which he participated. Murdered by Ogaden Somalis in Jubaland 1900.
5. Ina Scott, sister of the missionary Peter Cameron Scott.
6. Sudanese troops had served faithfully and well for many years. Their work was arduous and continuous; constant expeditions separated them from their families for long periods. They were paid a pittance - trade goods worth 4 Rupees (5/4d) a month - much less than Swahili porters, and the pay was several months in arrears. The men's clothing was tattered, inadequate rations encouraged them to loot and plunder and they resented the frequent changes of officers, most of whom could only communicate through an interpreter. They realised that they were the force by which British rule was imposed in East Africa and as their sense of grievance grew, some of them believed they could rule Uganda themselves. Led by Bilal Effendi and Mabruk Effendi, some three hundred mutineers marched towards Kampala. They reached the fort at Lubia's, recruited the 100 man garrison, slew three British officers and prepared for a siege. After two months of siege and skirmish the mutineers escaped from the fort but were unable to reach the Sudanese garrison at Unyoro. Lieutenant E.G. Harrison overtook the rebels in the swamps of Lake Kioga and inflicted a decisive defeat on the Sudanese rebels. The Uganda mutiny collapsed.
7. Department store in Bayswater, London.

Chapter 8

Home leave. March 1898 - October 1898

In a little over two years the Uganda Railway had advanced a third of the distance to Lake Victoria. Criticism was voiced in Parliament about its slow rate of progress and its escalating cost. Consequently the Uganda Railway Committee in London commissioned Sir Guilford Molesworth, a consulting engineer, to inspect the line and report on its progress.

In East Africa the railway dominated the landscape, the economy, the labour force, the food supply and the conversation. Technically and logistically its construction posed a series of formidable challenges, and while the railway was everywhere acknowledged as an engineering tour de force, it was attacked for its poor organisation and its conspicuous lack of cooperation with the administration. Sir Charles Eliot, Commissioner of the Protectorate from 1900 to 1904, recalled this weakness in his book, "The East Africa Protectorate."

"Everybody is probably aware that the Uganda Railway has been the object of much criticism. It must be confessed that it was built with great technical skill, but otherwise in a somewhat singular and unbusinesslike manner. The construction was supervised by a committee sitting in the Foreign Office, composed of distinguished gentlemen of wide experience, but in most cases that experience did not embrace railway work....By a most unfortunate arrangement, the local administration of the railway was made entirely separate from the administration of the protectorate, although it included a great many things which really had nothing to do with railway construction, such as the policing and sanitation of the whole line and of the most important stations on it, and the management of the railway zone, a tract of 1 mile on each side of the line. The committee in their final report blandly remark that their arrangements insured harmonious working between the authorities of the protectorate and the officers of the railway. As a matter of fact they ensured a permanent squabble between the two administrations, which was most disadvantageous to the public interest and most unnecessary....Not only were the two administrations distinct, but the Uganda Railway Committee was not the same as the African Department in the Foreign Office; and it was said that the differences of opinion between the two were real and important. The result of all this was that whenever there was a question affecting both the railway and other interests in the protectorate, there was no common authority who could settle it except the Secretary of State. And, as the Secretary of State had clearly only time to acquaint himself with questions of the utmost gravity, this meant that no one quite knew who decided all the questions of moderate importance. Hence much confusion."

In England Francis Hall and Beatrice Russell were married. In preparing for their life together at Fort Smith, no doubt they went shopping together in London for a wardrobe suitable for a lady to wear in equatorial Africa. The Army and Navy store was a popular outfitter, though Burberry supplied the better quality clothes. The main object was to protect the wearer from the harmful vertical rays of the sun and red material was believed to give good protection. A hat was an essential item of wear in Africa from seven in the morning until sunset. The choice was either a large beehive-shaped solar topi made of cork, or a large-brimmed double terai built of two thicknesses of heavy felt and lined with red flannel to protect the complexion. Bee would also have chosen a heavy divided skirt made from thorn proof material and a long-sleeved, high-necked, white or khaki tailored blouse worn under a coat with a fitted spine pad lined with red felt. Stays, stockings, breeches and high, stout leather boots completed the outfit.

They sailed for Mombasa in September 1898.

Chapter 9

GATHERING MUSHROOMS BY MOONLIGHT

Mombasa. 6.10.98

My Dear old Dad,
    Just a line to let you know we arrived all safe. Bee stood the voyage very well, but the heat & the slight tossing we got coming down the coast upset her a bit. However she is very fit now & a rest here for a few days is doing a world of good. I am awfully busy getting things ready for the march up. I was very lucky in Zanzibar for I managed to get four good horses at fairly reasonable rates and today they landed here alright.
    The Railway is now at Kiboko River, 21 miles beyond Kibwezi, so we get over the worst of the march & only have about 7 days march to Kikuyu. All our baggage arrived alright & everything has gone splendidly up to date. Bee is very favourably impressed with the place so far, & all the people in Zanzibar & here received us royally & have been awfully kind. We are inundated with invitations & have our time pretty well occupied & Bee is in splendid spirits. I have found a beautiful Arab horse for her which I hope will live. No time for more as I must go & see after the horses.

Kikuyu. Nov. 7th '98.

I am thankful to say that Bee is in perfect health, & though we have not been able to settle in to the house yet and are still in tents, we hope to be more comfortable in a day or two. The whole District & Station are in a terrible state & it will take me months to get the place straight again, but I hope it will all come right in time.

We were met by very sad news at the coast. Poor Cooke, who was one of my Assts. when I left; a Capt. in the Canadian Arty. & a friend of Linney Wadmore, was shot dead by old Dugmore in a sudden mad fit. Dugmore is now undergoing trial at Mombasa, & though he is absolutely mad, I hope he will be hung. Then later we heard that poor Harrison of the Railway, one of the three who gave me the watch, had been mauled by a lion & four days later died from blood poisoning & shock after amputation of the right arm. This was terrible news, for he was one of my best chums & he was the only man in E. Africa that Bee knew. We now have Nelson, Haslam[1] and Harrison buried in our garden.

EXTRACT OF LETTER FROM BEE HALL TO MISS MIN HALL.

Kikuyu. Nov.6. 1898

I was not sorry to leave Mombasa which we did on October 13th. Thank goodness, say I, that 214 miles of Rly. are finished. I would have hated going through the Taru desert; 14 days safari work for me was quite enough. We did about 136 miles of marching. I don't think any description of the Taru desert can describe what it is like; hundreds and hundreds of miles of scrub, and all as if it had been powdered with flour. The cactus grows to an immense height, 20 ft high, but all covered with this white dust. It's most curious to go by all these miles & see thousands of trees with no leaves on, all as if dead, not a sign of green anywhere.

Frank spotted two lions, or rather a lion & a lioness; everyone in the carriage saw them but myself; I was sorry. At one place along the line called Tsavo, 22 men had been killed by these brutes and there was a regular panic amongst the men working on the Railway. I do think the Railway is much misrepresented. It is most comfortable with nice broad seats going the length of the carriage, as in India. We stopped at Voi for the night and slept in the carriage, and I enjoyed it as it was very cool & no mosquitoes which Mombasa had. The next night we slept at Melindi, a very dirty spot where we dined with Mr. Carpmall, who came out with us, & the following morning we reached rail-head, a filthy place for dirt & dust, red lava as fine as flour, and as a wind gets up every evening, you can imagine the state we and all our things were in. We dined with a Mr. Spooner, a rather dull gent. After dinner I sat in a long chair and, I am sorry to say, went fast asleep. I fear I shall not be asked again to dine with Mr. Spooner!

We stayed [at railhead] until Monday before starting our upcountry march. Sunday night we heard a lion roar and I suppose one of the horses did too, as it bit itself free of its halter & raced up & down in the darkness. Frank was out of bed like a shot and he & the syce were a long time catching him. I confess I was in a deadly fright inside the tent. He was caught at last and the lion moved on to another quarter of the camp. Then a hyaena began to lift his voice. I was not happy!!

Everything has been allowed to go to pieces while Frank has been in England; the rooms not even cleaned so I live in a tent.

Letter from Francis Hall to his father.

Kikuyu. 17. 1. '99.

Just a hurried stave before leaving on another expedition. I am a grass widower here today, for Bee went off on 13th. with her brother Edward to stay at Machakos until I return in about 10 days time. Edward was at Machakos when he got a telegram with the sad news of his father's death. He started at 3.15 a.m. the following morning & marched to Nairobi,[2] 39 miles, by 5 p.m. There he borrowed a horse & rode on here. It was a terrible blow for Bee, but having Ted here made things easier. I had to go off on 13th & only got back yesterday, so Bee would have had a very lonely time with her own thoughts & anxieties about me, had she stayed here. So off she went with Edward & will stay until I go to fetch her. Justice, who is in Command of the troops with me, has left his wife there too, so Bee will have company....Bee has been awfully fit ever since she arrived; in fact both of us are as fit as can be. I hope to get the District properly settled & then we shall have an easier time. At present rather too much work & consequently see very little of Bee in the daytime except at meals.

Kikuyu. March 1st. '99.

I don't think I have written since we returned from the great expedition against a portion of the Wakikuyu some 40 miles away from here who had been indulging in the slaughter of some Swahilis just before I returned from England....We left Kikuyu with about 150 rifles & a following of about 3000 natives, but this crowd was too unmanageable so I sent most of them off to their homes, only keeping about 500. We marched over the mountain to the west to avoid friendly country & after four days emerged from the bamboo forest & came down into the enemies' country. We slept one night at an altitude of 8300 ft. & the cold was intense; six blankets were none too much over one, & how the men managed I fail to understand....As usual the natives had deserted their villages & bolted with all their livestock. However we scoured the forest & collected a good deal & then proceeded to march quietly through the country, sending columns out to burn the villages & collect goats &c. We very rarely saw any of the people; when we did they were at very long ranges so we did not have much fun, but we destroyed a tremendous number of villages & after fourteen days emerged on the plains of the East Ward, having gone straight from one end to the other of the disaffected districts. We captured altogether some 10,000 goats & a few cattle & this on top of the previous expedition must have been a severe blow to them. Justice & I had a pretty hard time, for one of us had always to be on guard at night; so we took turns & the result was we averaged about 4 hours sleep a night & had 9 hours in the saddle every day, & what with building a kraal every night for the goats & bridging every river we came to, the fourteen days were quite enough for both of us & we were glad to get back.

I went down to the Athi to meet Bee & brought her back. One of the fellows at Machakos brought her to the Athi, so she came through from Machakos to here, 47 miles, in two days which was pretty hard work. I got sore eyes from the dust kicked up by goats & the glare, the first time I have ever suffered in that way, but the heat just now is trying, & owing to the long drought, everything is parched up.

Macdonald and all his expedition turned up here all well & we had a great talk over old times. The Uganda business seems as complicated as ever, & as they are withdrawing all the Indian troops, there is every chance of further trouble before long....

....There are rumours that we shall soon be having big changes out here. Hardinge goes home on leave in April & it is probable we shall get a new

Chief. I must say I shall not be sorry, for the present way of running the show is nothing more than "marking time." We should never get any forrader in a century. The Railway is now about 60 miles from us, creeping on slowly. It will pass within 1 & a half miles of the Fort & goes over the route that Blackett & I found. They have started earthworks up on the mountains & the Wakikuyu are working splendidly at it....

....I received the three boxes of trees from Sawbridge Worth; they were beautifully packed, but unfortunately we were delayed at the coast which did not improve them. Most of the trees are alright I think, but the raspberries, currants and gooseberries have suffered severely & I am afraid I shall lose most of them. I have put them all in the ground under cover, & have them well watered, but the garden is as dry as a chip so I must wait until the rains come to plant them out.

Kikuyu. 1st. April. 1899.

I can't quite understand why you were left so long without news of us for I wrote on 13th Jany. from here, on 16th, & again when I came back from my expedition early in February....Yours of 24th Feby. reached me yesterday; they are delayed some days at the coast, about which I am making a row.

You mention Bee's accident with her horse. It was trying to climb up an almost perpendicular bank out of a stream & just as it got its forefeet on top, the hind legs sank in the mud & over he went. Bee got an awful ducking but was luckily unhurt, some of my men pulling her out very smartly. The Wallaces are still here, the McQueens at Nairobi, about 8 miles off. We have quite a large party here now, & as the railway approaches, of course the community will be increased....

....We are still in the Fort & likely to be for some time, as owing to the drought, building has been out of the question. However Bee has made our rooms so jolly pretty & comfortable that old hands don't recognize the old shanty, & our bedroom beats anything of the kind in these parts. I have ordered a lot of material on Govt. a/c for the new house, & now the rains are commencing, hope to get on with it. We had wonderful luck with all our belongings, even the dinner service which Murton gave us arriving here without a crack in anything. But the triumph of transport was the piano which reached here without a scratch in it & in splendid tune. Bee was very delighted & it gets plenty of exercise every evening. Bee works hard all the morning at housework &c. and takes a rest in the afternoon before visitors arrive. In the evening we generally get out for half an hour's stroll around, & back to a little music & dinner at 7.30....

....Things in Uganda are anything but satisfactory & I should not be surprised at any moment to hear the whole country was in an uproar. I wish they would have an enquiry into the whole show, perhaps things might go on better. I am getting more work here than I know what to do with, & as they go on piling up the office work, we get little chance of visiting our Districts & the natives will soon get out of hand if we do not watch them. Most of my native police &c. have blossomed out into traders & though they stick to the old District they are not in my garrison. The old order changeth & we are now almost dependent on local labour. To my mind they are simply courting disaster by trying to run the show as if it was a part of India instead of a country about 2000 years behind India or any other place. We are trying to race before we can walk & one of these days we shall bring up with a round turn, as Uganda has, & shall then have to start afresh. At present we are ordered to make revenue anyhow & our returns will probably look wonderful on paper. But seeing that most of this is made out of their own officers - I have paid fully 450 Rupees myself one way or the other - & before a native can invoke the aid of justice, he must pay up fees, it is hardly one's idea of administering a country or protecting natives.

Major Smith has chucked up his job in disgust & a good few others would like to if they could afford it. Fancy, we have never had a paper or a magazine since we came out except from friends, I paid a man named Blair on the Royal Exchange a year's subscription for several papers &c. Whether he sends them to the wrong address or never sends them at all I know not. We never get them....The rains have begun at last & it is very bleak & cold.

Kikuyu. April 12th 1899

I am having an awful time just now, nothing but office work, answering silly dispatches. Bee is as fit as can be, but of course as I can't get out, she does not have much fun. However I hope, when once I get over the office work up to the end of March, we shall be able to go for a week's picnic & see a bit of the country....

....We are having lovely weather now, rain at night & most perfect sunshiny days. Bee is in love with the piano, which is a beauty & greatly appreciated by everybody. The Railway is still about 60 miles off but we hope to see it here before we start home again. I shall have an awful time when the Indians come into the District but hope to have more clerks & another Assistant. We have just had a Doctor appointed, an Irishman & a very good chap.

Kikuyu. April 25th 1899.

    I am getting run off my head with worry & work, though it is now 11.15 p.m. & Bee has gone to bed long ago. I have only just finished a batch of official despatches. I am afraid they are all "bilious effusions" to Ainsworth & now a deputation of Wakikuyu have come in to report that some Masai youngsters have broken into their huts & stolen sheep, so I must send some men off to investigate. The Wakikuyu have killed one, I am glad to say, for I think they are four incorrigibles who broke away from gaol yesterday & I shall hope to catch the three tomorrow.

    My Assistant Lloyd[3] is at Machakos being prosecuted for "wrongful confinement" of a Goanese who calls himself a Portuguese subject. He & Lloyd had a few angry words & Lloyd told the police to take him into the Fort. My men are so accustomed to collar a man & put him into the gaol that when they got the chance at a Goanese, whom they hate, they promptly chucked him in amongst the natives. He was allowed out almost at once, but of course seeing the chance of heavy damages, prosecuted Lloyd. Ainsworth is quite non-plussed with an advocate arguing on each side. The result is Lloyd has been away three weeks & likely to be some more yet.

    The principal news here is the arrival of Boy Russell & young Haggard. They are both very fit & like this part of the country. I have advised them to settle near here & start a market garden as there is plenty of money to be made now that the Railway is approaching & they are negotiating for land & hope to start at once....

    ....Did I mention that Ainsworth told us that he & I had been recommended for an honour? I don't think it worth very much if he gets it, for he did nothing for Uganda, whereas the onus of all the transport work, both for MacDonald & the troops, fell on me. However if it helps one on, I shan't be sorry to get a C.M.G. or some acknowledgement for a lot of worry & anxiety, to say nothing of the risks we ran when we relieved Naivasha & the Ravine. We up-country men get very little thanks & no increase of pay, whereas the coast men, who are mostly junior to us, get their pay increased & houses built for them &c. which is rather annoying. I haven't grumbled yet but shall have to soon if they give all the plums to the coast men & forget us senior men who have been in the interior all our time & consequently have not the ear of the Consul-Genl.

    We are all in hopes that the protectorate will be amalgamated now that the railway & telegraph have got so far. We shall then have one experienced boss, like Sir Marshall Clarke who was in Basutoland, who being new, will assess men on their merits & not on what they tell him themselves of their former achievements.

Bee is as happy as a mudlark. We were out tonight long after sundown gathering mushrooms by moonlight. The climate suits her splendidly & she has quite fallen in with the life. The piano of course is a great source of pleasure, but after all she does not get very much time to practice, for she does household work all the morning, & with a slight rest & writing, the afternoon soon passes, & as we generally have guests to dinner she makes odds & ends of dainty dishes & is always the busy Bee. We are still in the old quarters for the good reason that the Govt. won't give us any money to build others, & not being millionaires we cannot afford to spend money on Govt. buildings. Fancy they have spent 60 to 80,000 Rupees on each house at the coast for the Treasurer & other officers, even providing furniture, down to fairy lamps for the dinner table, & we can't get a house, much less furniture. However our rooms are the prettiest & most comfortable up-country & it is great fun to hear the old hands compare the present state with the past. One said the other day, "Hang it! I must take my hat off," as he entered the dining room, which rather gave away the old habits....

....We are having splendid rains & the country is beautifully fresh & green. I am busy putting in garden seeds, though as I never get out of the office until dark, I have to trust entirely to my native gardener.

Kikuyu. Aug 15th '99.

I'm afraid it is some time since I last wrote but I have had a pretty battling time of it with all the Railway camps scattered through my District, keeping the peace between the natives & the coolies. I was amused at your remarks about the coolies as a peaceful law-abiding lot. The crowd they have out here are the scum of India, mostly refugees from justice, & being in such numbers, often 4000 in a camp, they think they can do as they like with the Jungle Wallahs; so they raid & steal whenever opportunity offers & it is almost impossible to bring a charge home to any particular men. However I am glad to say that the first time they attempted a raid on the Wakikuyu the natives drove them into camp, wounding one man slightly with a poisoned arrow. This put the fear of goodness into the coolies & since then we have had no trouble beyond a few petty thefts. The Railway is pushing on & I hope in about 3 months will be out of my District & into Uganda Territory

& I shall be very glad if they get through without any rows.

We gave them a great Champagne Lunch to celebrate the advent of the Railway. All the people in Kikuyu joined in, but of course the chief part fell on us. Bee ran the whole thing & we had a most sumptuous spread; salmon & lobster salads & various other kinds of salads, beef, beef steak pie, partridges, hams, tongues, fowls &c. fruit salads, blancmanges, shapes, jellies, tarts, custards, & all sorts of luxuries; in fact nothing of the kind has ever been seen in Kikuyu before. The tables looked awfully pretty with heaps of flowers & a plentiful display of our silver & plate. We had a large marquee pitched, draped with flags, a horse-shoe table & 30 sat down including 5 ladies.

We made a day of it; first a shooting match, Kikuyu vs Railway & they beat us by four points, this before lunch. Afterwards we were all photographed & all signed the visitors' book which is now closed as we can't have globe-trotters & Railway passengers mixed up with the Old Pioneers. Then I had called up a lot of Wakikuyu to give a native dance which proved a most interesting game to them all, for of course the Railway people had never seen it. In the evening we divided all the guests out amongst residents for dinner & afterwards all assembled again in our old dining room for a smoking sing-song which was a grand success, & as it was the first event of the kind since the Railway left Mombasa, was greatly appreciated.

The Railway gave a return picnic last Sunday & ran a special train for it, but unfortunately I was laid up in bed, so neither Bee nor I could go, for Bee didn't care to go without me. I have had rather a bad time for the last fortnight with an abscess on my right shin; the Doctor calls it periostitis. The whole thing started by my going down to Nairobi, about 8 miles on a trolley with the Doctor & his wife. It is all down hill so we simply flew down, & after doing our business we were foolish enough to stay to dinner with one of the Railway men & eventually left for home at 11 p.m. The men of course had to shove the whole way which was a slow job. It rained the whole way, & as I had lent my mackintosh to Mrs. Waters, I got a pretty good drenching. This gave me a chill on the liver & after a few days I had to go to bed with rather a sharp bout of my old enemy, fever & ague. At the same moment my shin got very sore & developed a magnificent abscess about as big as a cricket ball. The Doctor chuckled hugely at getting me under his knife, & as he is a great advocate for bed for all ailments, I have now been 14 days in bed & am today in a long chair against the Doctor's orders, but I told him I couldn't stay in bed any longer.

We are having the most extraordinary weather just now, bitterly cold & Scotch mists every day until about 1 o'clock. I don't know what is coming over the country. The crops in Machakos District have failed for want of rain, & the starving Wakamba are scattered all over the country robbing everywhere. A good few Wakikuyu who neglected their fields are dying of starvation & to make matters worse they have sent us the small-pox from Mombasa. We luckily caught the latter in time, & by stringent regulations we have managed so far to keep it within bounds. There are about 100 cases in the isolation camp & about a dozen have died. Thank goodness the natives are so frightened of it that they carefully keep away from all camps, so we have had no cases amongst them so far. But in Mombasa I hear it is awful; cases of confluent smallpox walking about in the bazaar & every day the police pick up dead bodies in the streets. In one day they picked up 57, yet nobody seems to care, & natives are allowed to come up-country freely by train. It is time we had some strong man to boss this country; things are simply going from bad to worse, & goodness knows where they will end. I wish Sir Harry Johnstone[4] had been put over the whole show instead of only over Uganda. I have had a letter from the Foreign Office thanking me for my service to Lt. Col. MacDonald's expedition & also one from the Chief Engineer on behalf of the Railway Committee thanking me for having arranged all the land purchase through my District with the natives. These letters are very satisfactory in a way but I would much rather have an increase of pay. We had an Asst. Engineer on the Railway up here named Fawkes; his cousin is one of the Secretaries to Uncle George. He is a very nice fellow & tells me that he hopes to be able to get on the Administrative of the Protectorate. It is about time we recruited a few more gentlemen into the show.

Hardinge being at home, Craufurd is acting for him. He is most cordially hated by everyone at the coast, though I must say I always get on well with him. The result is they are all fighting & squabbling, chiefly about precedence & brass buttons, & the country is going to the dogs.

At present we have 12 C.M.S. Missionaries here in quarantine. Leakey is the only old hand & he has brought a wife[5] with him this time. I have seen three out of the six ladies & they are certainly a vast improvement on any previous samples of the genus. They are ladies & they seem very jolly, so Bee has had one or two enjoyable tea fights.

Kikuyu. Aug. 21st '99.

If your weather is anything like we are having just now, it will be lovely. We have cloudy, cold mornings, but about 11 the sun comes out & it is just perfect. Bee & I are sitting on the verandah writing, & as old Pine of Hadlow would say "it's worth arf-a-crown to be alive."

Jackson has just come back from leave & is spending a day or two here. He brings the good news that Berkeley, late Commr. in Uganda & formerly our boss in the Coy. has been appointed to Tunis. This will suit him much better than Uganda as it enables him to have his wife & child with him. We hear Hardinge is coming out again & the sooner the better, for at present every Dept & every Officer is fighting the other. There are rumours that I am to be moved further North amongst the Wakikuyu, but I doubt if we shall get enough money in the Estimates to be moved & erect a new Station.

Small-pox is spreading slowly in spite of all our efforts, & at last has got into my jail which is rather a nuisance as I have an average of over 60 prisoners.

My leg is nearly well & I manage to hop around a bit in spite of Doctor's orders to the contrary & hope to be quite fit in a day or two. Then I must run up along the line & see that everything is alright & afterwards Bee & I are off for a few days picnic in the wilds where we shall get some shooting & fishing.

Boy Russell has just accepted a temporary billet with the Uganda Transport to look after their section in the Kedong Valley, about 28 miles from here. I think this is the best thing he can do pro tem. He has had no experience & is somewhat lacking in the self confidence necessary to enable him to start anything on his own account. He has made many schemes but never made a start, & as he is not quick at picking up the language, is rather handicapped. So I hope a month or two of regular work will help him along & it is just possible it may lead to something better. We had a Roman Catholic bishop up here the other day, a very jolly old chap. He is going to build a hospital & make a garden. There are 12 Missionaries here quarantined en route for Uganda & tonight we are going to have 3 of them to dinner. So Bee has been making tarts & other dainties in her Rippingille stove, which by the bye has proved most useful.

The Railway had a nasty accident the other day. One of the temporary bridges built of sleepers caught fire & was burnt down. A train came along at night & crashed through the whole thing. Luckily the train was only laden with material & the driver, stoker & guard jumped off & did not get hurt. However it blocked all traffic for five days so our mails were very late.

Kikuyu. Oct. 17th. '99.

I was so sorry to hear from Min that you thought I was very remiss in writing. I suppose I have really been so, but between Bee & myself I think you have been kept fairly well up in our doings. To tell the truth I wish pens & ink had never been invented. I spend the whole of my time now in the office slinging ink, & then never seem to be able to keep up with the work. Ainsworth, who is now living only 8 miles off, gave me 19 despatches in two days, & has accomplished 380 since the beginning of the year. Besides these we have the Treasury Dept. who never seem to understand the simplest entry in the a/cs but must write queries. The Judicial Dept. who want to know, when a man is convicted of stealing goats, whether he stole 50 or 51; or in another case, of sugar stealing, whether the sugar was white or brown & such like nonsensical questions which all require a lot of work in the shape of reference to the evidence, which also has to be written out in full. In fact things have come to such a pass that life is hardly worth living & I wish I could see my way to get another billet & get clear of all this idiotic, snobbish, brass button & uniform business, so-called an Administration, where not a single Officer up-country has ever been 20 miles from his Station & we know less about the natives than we knew seven years ago.

As for the Administration we have been cut down to the uttermost farthing to make allowances for a toy Army which never does anything but drill & blow bugles, while the Officers have a State-aided shooting trip & if anything crops up get medals & D.S.O.s. The whole show is very sickening but I hope that when Hardinge comes out & hears our opinions of things there may be a change. Our present Actg. Commr., having been a Sergt. in a line Regt. has no soul above brass buttons & saluting & of course it is quite impossible to expect him to grasp the gravity of the situation....

....We rode to Nairobi to visit our Railway friends & had a hearty welcome as they always come here. They are really an awfully nice lot of people & it is a treat for Bee to get out now & again to see ladies, though she, like me, is very happy & contented in our own little cow-house, & though they all have very swagger bungalows which the Govt. won't allow us, they cannot beat our little shanty for cleanliness & snuggery, for Bee makes the best of everything, & though our quarters are small they are awfully snug & comfortable & I shall be sorry to leave the old "Castle perilous," as MacDonald called it in his book.

Fancy our being inundated by Lords, live ones!! I was never so astonished in my life as when I saw young Lord Basil Blackwood (who travelled up in the train with us last year) walk into the Fort with another man, Lord Alexander Thynne & mildly remark that he had come out for a short shooting trip & had been to Khartoum since he saw us last. They stayed to lunch & we had a jolly chat. Thynne is a son of the Marquis of Bath of Longleat. Fancy, us with two Lords at lunch & Delamere will be here in a few days. We shall soon qualify for the aristocracy!....

....I have an awful job on now with the famine & the smallpox. I have an average of 370 famine stricken people to feed daily. It is the most pitiful job I have ever had. Poor beggars, owing to drought their crops failed; as a matter of fact the Uganda Relief Expdn. took all their reserve food & now they are in a pitiful state; not all, but the poorer people who live entirely on the proceeds of their land. A large fund has been raised out here to assist, but when one considers that the Govt. is feeding thousands at Mombasa, 1500 at Kibwezi, 1500 at Machakos, while I have 370 here, all our efforts are very puny. If Min could see her way to raise only a few pounds of Famine Fund it would be a grand thing. Every man in the country is getting subscriptions to help, & I think Tonbridge ought to be in it with all its connections with these parts.

No one could describe the frightful misery & horrors of this famine. Out of 370 of my camp, 200 are children; in fact my numbers today are 169 children, 60 women with children at breast, 56 women, 26 men. The rains have just commenced, so that yesterday & today many have returned to their homes to plant. We are thousands of Rupees over our allowances. We could not send them away starving, though we were advised the funds were expended, so we took it on ourselves & went on feeding them. I started a subscription amongst the other Wakikuyu 3 days ago & have already got 60 goats worth 240 Rupees & hope to get at least 150 goats in the next week which at least proves that the richer class of natives appreciates our efforts & is willing to assist his poorer compatriots, a trait which is not always found in native Africans....

....Small-pox is rampant & I have a camp of about 25 to 30 patients, but thank goodness I have a Medical Officer to look after this who vaccinates everyone on sight & insists on them parading on the eighth day to get the lymph for others....Things were so bad, I had to see the smallpox corpses buried & visit the hospital & so on, so that Bee & I were vaccinated as a matter of precaution. It took well on both of us & we had a bad time of it, but now it is over I feel very thankful that it is done. What with famine & small-pox we are burying 6 or 8 a day. One can't go for a walk without falling over corpses. However the rains have now commenced & please God the worst of our troubles are over. While writing this tonight the food supply arrived & I had to go & serve it out & it is really pretty awful to have to select the living & lay aside the corpses with one's own hand. The natives won't touch a corpse, in fact have to be coerced to bury the dead. So if one wants to get through the job, one must drag out the corpses oneself or wait for hours. I am not squeamish, but barring the burying of the dead of Grant's caravan, this is the worst job I have tackled....

....This service now is hardly bread & butter. In fact if things go on as at present we shall never be able to afford to get home on leave. Living is so frightfully expensive, & economize as we will, it takes us all our time to pay the insurance money (which amounts to two months pay) & keep clear of debt. Every other man in the service is head over ears in debt & the whole show is rotten from stem to stern. We want a good man at the helm. Until we get one, life is not worth living & I should be jolly glad to get out of it; but of course it is our bread & butter & even if the butter is rancid we must put up with it. And now my dear old Dad, having fed the hungry, written my fingers stiff, & grumbled to the full extent of an Englishman's privilege, I must shut up.

Machakos. Nov. 26th. '99

As you will see by the address I have at last been ousted from Kikuyu & am now stationed here. This is the next best Station to Kikuyu, but at the same time I am awfully sick at having to leave the old quarters. The fact is that headquarters are now at Nairobi, only 8 miles from Kikuyu, so there was no use of me there, & as there is no money in the Estimates for a new Station, I was moved. I was ordered first to go to Kitui, but as this is a very out-of-the-way place & very unhealthy, I objected & was sent here. The amazing part is that the real reason for the move is jealousy on Ainsworth's part. We were much too friendly with the Railway people, & as A. & his wife are rather barred by all, he did not like it & so got the move arranged. But Sir Arthur Hardinge will be out in a few days & then I am going to talk the matter over with him & see what he says.

We have a bigger house here, with zinc roof, but it is not nearly as cheerful as Kikuyu, & as for the people of the country, the Wakamba, I hate the sight of them.

Our Actg. Chief, Craufurd, goes home on leave directly Hardinge comes back, & as he has been practically convicted of fraud by the High Court, we shall probably be rid of him for good. If we can only get rid of A. now, life may be worth living again. These fellows, brought up behind a counter, get too big for their boots & make life quite unbearable for others. It doesn't do to be a gentleman, especially if at all popular, in these parts.

We had a most awful job packing up to come away, but luckily I managed to borrow two donkey carts & loaded the piano, crockery &c. on them, & by looking after them myself on the road, everything came through alright which was great luck. The piano is still in first rate order & I hope when we have done the house up we shall be fairly comfortable.

Poor old Fort Smith is to be evacuated shortly, so one of the old landmarks will disappear. A. is centralizing all the staff & the work at Nairobi, & the general opinion is that there will be big trouble. However he is the great "I am" at present, so we must obey & sit tight until Hardinge arrives. Here we have the Headquarters of the military with three Officers & a Doctor so we have a little Community of our own, but we are 23 miles from the Railway which makes living expensive, though relieves one of a deal of correspondence & telegrams.

We have had heavy rains which have made the country green & bright but it is not a pretty place. The Fort is shut in a horseshoe of hills & in front the rolling plains with a few bare hills scattered about. However it is a good climate & one can get some shooting around so we shall make the best of it.

Machakos. Dec. 20th 1899.

Our Xmas this time is somewhat saddened by recent events, as it was last year. The other day poor Capt. Godfrey, O.C. troops here, & an awfully nice fellow, went out shooting with Stayner, a Lieut. of the E. African Rifles. They were camped about 15 miles from here & Godfrey went out & wounded a lion close to camp. He went back & called Stayner & they each went up separate gullies to look for the wounded beast. Each had some Nubian soldiers with him besides two gun-bearers. Godfrey came up on the beast & fired with his 8 bore elephant gun, but he was evidently excited as both bullets struck too far back, through the stomach. Then he fired two shots with a 12 bore rifle but apparently missed both, as there were no marks in the skin. The lion then charged. Godfrey's gun-bearer apparently gave him the 8 bore empty, for it was very stiff & he had been unable to open & load it. Both gun-bearers retired & the lion jumped on to Godfrey, mauling his right hand & arm & seizing him by the right side, shaking & throwing him about like a rat. His right leg was also bitten. The Nubians rushed in, & being frightened to fire, beat the beast with the butts of their rifles, with the result that he left Godfrey & struck down a Nubian, mauling him badly. At last a man put a bullet through the animal's head & settled him.

Poor Godfrey was carried into his camp insensible about 3 p.m. The news reached us here at 7 p.m. & at once the Doctor, "Mann" & a Lieut. Osborne left in drenching rain on a pitch dark night, & after floundering along the native path, reached the camp at 5 a.m. Mann at once put Godfrey under chloroform, as he was in such pain he could not bear being moved, & examined him. He found the teeth had not penetrated the abdomen but he was fearfully lacerated & bruised, & though he came to about noon & was fairly cheerful & bright, a reaction set in & he died of shock, but in no pain, at 4.30 p.m., only 25 hours after he had been mauled. He was brought in & buried here with full Military Honours next day at 3 p.m. so that the whole thing was over in 48 hours.

Two companies of troops, a detachment of police, all the Europeans, Greeks, Goanese, Indians & a good many of the coast natives in the settlement attended the funeral which was very well carried out.

It has been rather a blow to Bee, for though she had not seen much of him, still he was talking with us a few hours before he left, & it brought it close home to see his body carried back in our hammock. This makes the third European killed by lions since Bee & I came out & the official record for the Uganda Railway for last year was 38 coolies killed by lions, not a bad list.

This place at present is beautifully green & consequently very pretty, but Bee does not like the change from Kikuyu. There are no ladies here; the wife of my cashier, sister of Mrs. Ainsworth, is the only woman in the settlement & she is of course no companion for Bee, though not a bad sort in her way....We have got the dining room very comfortable at last & the bedroom is fairly so, but owing to the small windows & brown clay walls, it is so dark & cheerless. Still we have been glad of the galvanized iron roof during the late heavy rains....

....Tell Min the "Daily Mails" are simply the joy of my life. The war news is grand reading & it is simply splendid to see how the colonies are hanging out in Mafeking & Kimberley. The slaughter is pretty awful but this must be expected with quick firing guns and the long range small-bore rifle. There will be many sad homes in England & the colonies this Xmas, but the fighting has been splendid & it is better to be killed in a good fight than to sit down like whipped curs, as Britishers had to in the South after '81. They ought to have Oom Paul & bury him in Gladstone's grave with the grand old muddler & keep an everlasting fire on top of them....

....Here I have no Assistant, which is a nuisance as I can't get away, but I have a European as cashier & a Goanese Clerk who is also Postmaster. Administration here is a farce. I carry on a large banking business with traders, sign vouchers, write Official letters in answer to others about nothing, & occasionally try a case of theft or a Civil case of debt. In the Criminal Cases the accused always pleads guilty because unless they are caught in the act they are rarely caught at all; while in debt cases the defendant almost invariably acknowledges the debt & calmly adds he has nothing to pay with. As for any connections with the natives or any knowledge of one's District, this is apparently a secondary consideration nowadays, for one can never get any relief from ink slinging, & if one was to leave the Station for a week, there would be enough accumulated clerical work to give anything but a type-writer scrivener's cramp. I suppose things will be placed on a better footing one of these days, but in the meanwhile we are having a poor time.

I have been charged an enormous accnt. for "expenses incurred in connection with Mrs. Hall's journey to Kikuyu with 34 loads," & I had to arrange with & pay extra people to fetch loads which had been left behind owing to desertion of porters, which cost several hundred Rupees. It is too aggravating for words. If this claim is upheld by Hardinge, I shall have paid more than a quarter of a year's pay to land in Mombasa & proceed to my Station, in Custom Duties & landing & transport charges, which is iniquitous. We have to pay Custom Duties on all clothing; we even had to pay on the small parcel May sent out the other day, & the fact of the matter is that four fifths of the revenue of the country is made out of the up-country Officers. Those at the coast get houses, furniture, even table linen & bedding free, whereas we not only have to provide our own, but pay Duty on it as well.

I saw Sir Harry Johnston & I think he has summed up things pretty well, for he remarked "it appears to me that all the money for this Protectorate is used up at the coast." So we have hopes that things may be put right, but we shan't recover monies paid out for Customs &c. An idea has come into my head that after the war there will be a lot of magistracies & other appointments to be given in the Transvaal. I should very much like to get a transfer & shall see if it cannot be arranged. Though of course rather rusty now, I used to talk the lingo like an Afrikander [sic]. I know the people, the country & the language, so ought to be qualified for a billet & should prefer it to the present state of so-called administration in these parts. However I must consider the best method of setting about it. I am looking forward to meeting Sir A. Hardinge & having a good talk with him....

....I am glad to say that with the good rains we have had, the crops are looking splendid. The famine camp which at one time contained over 1500 is now below 1000, I'm afraid chiefly owing to death, but still no others are coming in. Taking a rough average of the death rate in the famine camp it is estimated that considerably more than a third of the population of the District has died during the last 12 months.

Notes

1. Captain Arthur J. Haslam, BA, MD, FRCVS. Veterinary-Captain Haslam was inoculating cattle against rinderpest in the Nairobi area in July 1898 when he decided to join a punitive expedition against the Wakikuyu of Maluka who had killed some natives sent by the railway to buy food. Haslam allowed the expedition to start without him, and while trying to catch up with it, he and several of his porters were speared to death by Wakikuyu near Fort Smith.

2. The name Nairobi comes from the Maa language engore nyarobe, meaning the place of cold water. Francis Hall camped on the Nairobi River on the edge of the Kapiti Plains, ten miles from Fort Smith in June, 1893. In 1896 James Martin, the illiterate, Maltese born, British official spent ten days at Nyarobe river camp while recruiting African labour for the railway and in the same year Corporal George Ellis established a staging post for the pack animals used by Government. The site for the new railway headquarters, roughly halfway between Mombasa and Lake Victoria, had been chosen by George Whitehouse, Chief Engineer of the railway, when he made a reconnaissance of the route in 1897. It was simply the last stretch of level ground before the long climb to the lip of the Kikuyu escarpment followed by a precipitous descent and the subsequent traverse of the Great Rift Valley. When the rails arrived at mile 327 on May 30, 1899, Nairobi was no more than "a bleak, swampy stretch of soppy landscape," according to Ronald Preston, supervisor of the plate-laying gangs. It was an unhealthy site, plagued by mosquitoes and difficult to drain and soon after the arrival of the railway there was an outbreak of bubonic plague. All in all it was by no means an ideal location for the future capital of Kenya Colony, yet it suited the railway admirably.

3. Edward Lloyd, administrative officer.

4. Sir Harry Johnston, GCMG, KCB, appointed to the Special Commission to Uganda in 1899. Painter, naturalist, administrator.

5. Canon R. H. (Harry) Leakey married Mary Bazette.

Chapter 10

Nairobi, a tin-pot mushroom township

Machakos. Jany. 12th '00.

I must try to get off a few lines by tomorrow's mail, but really there is absolutely nothing to write about as we get no news of the outside world here except by mails & we haven't had an English mail for 20 days. We hear the P.&O. missed the connection with the B.I. at Aden for carrying contraband for South Africa. These minor details, together with the fact that a considerable portion of the Railway has been in a chronic state of "washed out" for the last month, have left us in blissful peace & ignorance of everything outside our own four walls.

We hear by wire that Craufurd & Ainsworth of this Prot., & Ternan, Mackinnon & Tompkins[1] of Uganda have been made C.M.G. in the New Year's Honours. There will be no holding A. now. I was recommended, but I suppose they take superior Officers first.

The most important news of all, as far as our particular show goes, is that we have had splendid rains. The crops are excellent & we hope very shortly to get rid of all the people in our famine camp. In fact today we have had a grand clearance; the Chiefs came in & took away fully two thirds of the mob & I hope tomorrow to get rid of more. We shall then only have forty or fifty left who require feeding up. Some of the Chiefs, having lost so many of their own people are only too glad to adopt any orphans we have to spare, so matters are coming right splendidly.

I am sorry to say there are bad accounts from Kikuyu. Since I left of course the natives have had practically no one to look to. The Nairobi show is purely a brass button, uniform, ink-slinging centre, so they have taken the bit in their teeth & have been making things hum a bit. In fact I hear it is quite unsafe for anyone to travel along the main road now, as highway robbery is an everyday occurrence. I am very sorry for the Wakikuyu; they are alright if they are looked after, but if left to themselves the old spirit will out.

Ainsworth sent here for troops the other day & an Officer & 50 men were sent to Fort Smith to patrol the road &c. It is rather a feather in my cap, though I feel so for the natives, who have never given much trouble when I have been amongst them, while every time I have gone away there has been trouble. When I was home in '95 the Kedong massacre took place & Dick was killed, & the place generally in a state of turmoil, & now when I am shifted to suit Ainsworth's private plans, the state of the District is worse than it has been for the last six years.

I am hoping to meet Hardinge shortly, when he comes up to Nairobi & talk things over with him. I hear now that Ainsworth is going home in April & there is no doubt he had me moved so that I should be out-of-the-way when he left, & so not be appointed to act in his place, but I think when I see Hardinge things will be put right.

Machakos. Feby. 25. '00.

Bee reminds me that the mail leaves for the coast tomorrow, so I must just put in a line to say we are fit & hope to have a run up to Nairobi next week to visit Sir Arthur & Lady Hardinge. There is little or no news here. We jog along in a peaceful way "the world forgotten & by the world forgot."

Machakos. March 16th 1900.

Here we are again after our little outing to Nairobi to see Sir Arthur Hardinge, so I must tell you all the news of our meeting. As you know I went up fully intending to have a good grumble at things in general & John Ainsworth in particular for the way I had been shifted from Kikuyu. I think Hardinge must have had an inkling that there was trouble in the wind, for the first thing he did when he jumped off his horse to speak to me, was to say, "we want you back amongst the Wakikuyu, Hall" & proceeded to expound the plan of opening up the Northern end of Kenia District & how I was to go & do it &c. &c. This rather took the wind out of my sails. However I got in my grumble in a polite sort of way & of course he put it down to his locum tenens, Craufurd, & said he had had nothing to do with it & all that sort of thing. I let him know what I thought of things generally & we parted the best of friends. The upshot is that we shall have to move again in a month or two & go into regular camp life for a time while we build a new Station, but we both like the idea, & though Hardinge said if I liked he would leave me here unmolested, I told him I would much rather get back to Kenia District amongst the Wakikuyu than stay here amongst these Wakamba who want a thorough good thrashing before anything can be made of them, they have been so spoilt by Ainsworth.

The move of course depends on the Estimates, but I don't think there is much doubt about it. It will be an awful bother & Bee will have to sell her piano, & other goods we shall store, doing with as little baggage as we can. Luckily Bee loves camp life, & as we shall only have about a year before coming home, it will not matter much.

From what Hardinge told me it will not be long before Uganda & this Protectorate are combined & then I hope things will go better. Hardinge is a wonderfully clever diplomat, but as an Administrator perfectly useless. He looks on everything as a huge joke, & as long as the revenue increases & everything slides along without any increase of expenditure, he is perfectly satisfied. The result is we are going on like Uganda did & gradually brewing heaps of trouble that will eventually cost thousands to put right, but of course Hardinge reckons his successor will come in for this, & in the meantime he takes the kudos for running the show economically.

At Nairobi, a tin-pot mushroom township, they have no less than five different law-courts. All the Magistrates live at their desks slinging ink, & the place is the most lawless and dangerous spot in Africa. Every night the police bombard indiscriminately with ball cartridge, & unless one is within stone walls, life is not worth 12 hours purchase. The night we arrived, Bee woke me & there was a regular fusillade going on; the police bugles sounded the alarm & there was a general hubbub. It turned out that the only result was that a poor wretched Indian trader, who was asleep in his bed in a tent in the bazaar, was shot dead. This led to a strike in the bazaar; all the shops closed & no one could get meat, bread or provisions, & they said they would not open again unless the Govt. looked after them properly.

A week before, the troops broke out & attacked a Somali camp; brisk firing went on for over an hour & the troops not only refused all orders, but actually broke into the guard room to obtain fresh supplies of ammn. to carry on the fight & only desisted when some 5 Somalis & 2 of the troops were killed & several wounded. This will give you some idea of what they call Administration at the Provincial Hdqrs. Despatches fly round by hundreds; if papers would do it, this would be the best governed country in the world. However one of these days, when the natives have wiped out a few Europeans, they may learn wisdom, & the only thing is to hope not to be amongst the first victims....

....The Railway is practically at a standstill, & during the last few months, owing to the heavy rains, has hardly run any trains. One bridge over the Stony Athi has been washed away five times in six weeks, & across the plains where it is nearly all black cotton soil, they have to dig out the rails after the train has passed over. It is awfully exciting travelling, but they go so slow, 4 miles an hour, that there is practically no danger. A truck runs off into the mud, they stop, dig it out, put it on the rails & go on. Near Nairobi there is an engine that took it into its head to go across country but got half-buried. They found it easier to build a fresh track round it than to get it back, so now the line dodges past the wreck & they are waiting for dry weather to put things straight. All this upper part of the line is temporary, hence the troubles. Their 3 million are finished at the end of this month & they are applying for two million more, & even with this they won't get through to the lake. I expect old Labby[2] will have plenty of copy on the subject....

....You will be delighted to hear that after all the correspondence & referring the matter to Sir A. Hardinge, we got off our transport bill with a cheque for something like 650 Rupees instead of 1300, a great saving. Still, when I look through my cheque book, I find I have paid more than a third of my pay to Govt. since I have been out, which is rather hard. The last a/c they sent me was for horse fodder, 1 Rupee 2 As., as there was no authority for such expenditure, though this was supplied when I had to rush off on service for 48 hours. Can you imagine H.B.M.'s Govt. being so petty?....

....Bee & I are both in rude health & very happy, barring petty John Ainsworth & transport worries, & we are going to retire to our new District & there sit tight & try to save money for a stupendous good holiday at home next year.

The new Station is to be as near the Sagana river as possible on the South side, under Kenia, so that I can get in touch with the natives all round to the North & East & at the same time be in touch with Nairobi, at a distance of about 70 miles. I have been through the country & have my diary with the names of all the Chiefs I met, so shall meet them as old friends, taking care by means of a wily interpreter to be able to fit the right names, such as "broken nose," "dented skull," "one eye," "one arm," and such like. So that by reading up my notes the night before, I can get along beautifully & they all feel flattered. I think we shall have a very jolly time though of course it will not be luxurious.

I have to pay my insurance next month which amounts to 2 months pay, & though we are living as quietly as possible, it seems that when we have paid all the Govt. demands & the insurance, we can only just manage to come clear of debt without saving anything for our holiday. Thanks to Bee's housekeeping our living costs very little; the Govt. is the greatest expense. A load of rice stolen out of store, in spite of sentries, I have to pay for. Anything lost on the Station must be paid for by the O.C. This comes very heavy when you can't even trust your own police.

March 17th. It is five years since I was mauled by the leopard. We are not going to have any celebration of it this time but shall get the others in for a rubber of whist this evening.

Machakos. May 29th 1900

Here we are again back in this place after a very rough & wet march to the neighbourhood of Mt. Kenia to select a site for our new Station. I must begin by telling you that as I write this I am sitting up with poor Bailey of the E. African Rifles who has had a fearful bout of Typhoid, & now has bronchitis & lung troubles on top of it. He has been on the verge of death for the last 3 days but thank goodness we have two Doctors looking after him & all take it in turn to sit up, & please God, if he gets through tomorrow, he is alright....
....We had a very hard safari, for the rain came down in torrents every night & the rivers were all in flood, & as we crossed no less than 22 in 31 days, you can imagine we had hard work. Some we crossed on rafts, some we bridged, & many we crossed over by native bridges, but as we had our horses, cows & donkeys, we had to swim them through everything. Accidents, thank goodness, were few considering we had 190 men, 3 horses, 2 cows with calves (for milk) & 4 donkeys. The wretched mokes were the worst in water; we drowned one on our way up & two more on the way home, & one calf died, but never lost a man.

Our horses did splendidly, but sad to relate, on my return I heard from Boy Russell at Kikuyu that the horse I had left with him was dead, & two days after our return my own pet horse "Beeswing," a white Arab, developed the regular South African horse sickness & died within 24 hours. He was a grand beast, & apart from the monetary loss, Bee & I mourn him as an old friend. The two horses cost us about 600 Rupees each up here & a sudden loss of £80 is a cruel blow. The Govt. gives us no allowance for horses, though we use them almost exclusively on service, but now we are left with only one pony between us & can't afford to buy another if we ever want to see home again. So we shall have to take turns on the way up to our new Station & once there do like all the rest, sit tight & do nothing, but take our leave when it comes due.

We found a lovely site for a Station, on a ridge about 30 miles South of the summit of Kenia. There is a small hollow on one side with a stream for drinking water, & on the other a deep ravine with a big river teeming with fish. The country is very like that around Fort Smith, very fertile, densely populated & the natives were very friendly. They well remember my last visit with Harrison in '96 & we were received well everywhere. We spent a night on the Tana River & I showed Bee all the sights there were to be seen. In spite of our troubles over the rivers &c., Bee thoroughly enjoyed the trip, & beyond a slight cough & cold, kept as fit as could be all through. I had a bout of fever on the road but got rid of it in a few days. We revelled in fish at every river; my few shillings worth of hooks judiciously distributed amongst a few men not only fed them, but provided the mess with breakfast & dinner.

The Officer (Stayner) who came in charge of the escort, got very seedy & was perfectly useless, either as an assistant or companion which was a pity. We should have done better, & been much happier without him. He had been through a course of bridging at some time in his career, theoretically, but he hadn't a practical idea in his head. When he came up against a full river, his Sergeant, an old Uganda Nubian ruffian was of infinitely more use, & his men were excellent when working under me. We started for a 20 day trip & got home in 31 days, so you may imagine we had some trifles to contend with en route. For five days we worked hard at one river, trying to bridge it, but every tree we threw across was carried away like matchwood. However at last we got some poles across in two spans & bridged it.

We found heaps of mail here on return & of course my desk was stacked with official effusions of the usual nonsensical order which will be attended to in due course if the ink holds out. We had a parade & a furious joy on the Queen's birthday but nothing else; with Bailey so bad no one felt like holding high revels, & the death of my horse did not add to my hilarity.

Poor little Lloyd, who was my Assistant in Kikuyu, died on 29th April in Nairobi of fever. I have not the slightest doubt it was typhoid, the same as Bailey's, though not recognized by the Doctors as anything but malaria. This has been a bad year & many old friends have gone & there is a fearful amount of sickness around. The wet season & sedentary life accounts chiefly, I think, for the lot.

I am allowed very little money to run & build my new Station, Rs. 12.000 for a whole year. This will not suffice for labour & police so we shall probably have a regular camp life for a time. However our leave is due in April next year so we know we have only 9 or 10 months of it to start with & shall make up our minds to make the best of it. The greatest blow to Bee is having to abandon the piano, but we can't possibly carry it, & to leave it with anybody means finding the ruins of it on one's return. The only thing is to sell it, keep the money, & pray for an Administrator who believes in keeping an Officer amongst people he knows & understands, & who have confidence in him. As long as we have men like Hardinge, who look on the job as a stepping stone to an Embassy & care nothing about the country, we shall never have any peace. And as was truly said, "you will draw your pay to live in a grass hut on a hill, taking your leave regularly every 20 months & doing nothing but answer absurd rot they send you, in the most humble & respectful spirit," & then they will wonder why they have mutinies & rebellions & have to spend millions to subdue natives, who if properly looked after, would never give any trouble.

Machakos. June 10th. '00.

Just a line to show that I am still alive & fit. We had a most awful shock last Sunday, getting a telegram to say that poor Edward Russell had died suddenly at Shimoni, his Station near "Wanga or Wassein" on the coast about 25 miles South of Mombasa.

He had been out on a trip, messing around swamps &c., & on his return was seized with violent vomiting & diarrhoea & died in his bed about 2 a.m. within 20 hours of his first attack. I can only imagine it was "heart". Bee suggests Cholera, but this has never been seen in Africa.... I never had such a shock as when I read the telegram & poor Bee was quite stunned. Luckily the Hindes are here, & Mrs. H. & Bee are great chums, so she has had someone to keep her company all day while I am in the office, & keep her from brooding too much over the sad loss of her pet brother. He was a great favourite with all & everybody mourns his loss.

I don't know what has come over the country. We have lost six men in six weeks & we only muster about 50, including the Railway Officers. Poor little Lloyd, lately my Asst. in Kikuyu, died at Nairobi; Weaver, an old Coy's hand & a great friend of mine, at Kismayu; & another man, Cummings, I had not met, also at Kismayu, probably from drinking bad water. Then we get news that Craufurd, our Senior Sub. Commr. died while at home on leave, & to cap everything, poor Ryall,[3] a great friend, who belonged to the Punjab Police & was Asst. Supt. of Police on the Railway, is yanked out of his railway carriage, when in bed sound asleep, by a beastly man-eating lion. Bee, I think, has told Min the story which is without exception the most marvellous lion story I have ever heard, but there is absolutely no doubt of the truth of it. A large party of Europeans has gone down to try & kill the beast.

Death generally takes three at a time out here, so now having taken a double share, we may hope for immunity for a short period. Craufurd's death creates the first vacancy amongst the Sub. Commrs. so there will probably be some moves & promotions, in which case I ought to be somewhere near, but with Hardinge one never knows what will happen. So we are not sanguine, but I expect our plans may be altered & am very anxious to hear how things are going to be arranged. Our patient, Bailey, a Lieut. of East African Rifles, has at last pulled round the corner, a marvellous recovery, for he got diphtheria after typhoid. But with two Doctors & careful nursing, & Bee & Mrs. Wilson cooking his food, he had better chances than most men get in this country. He has been on the verge of death for the last fortnight, but we took it in turns to sit up with him & watched every breath practically, day & night, & thank goodness managed to save him. He was awfully plucky & a splendid patient, but it was a very anxious time for us all.

Machakos. Aug. 5th 1900.

You will see that we are still at Machakos, but expect to leave anytime when my men & loads come up from the coast. Most of our things are ready packed & we intend to go up with nothing but camp kit, as we hope for leave next March or April. All our heavy stuff we are leaving here & our respectable clothing ready packed in boxes for the journey home. No further news has been received about the filling up of Craufurd's place, which might possibly mean an alteration in our plans; they are taking their time about settling the matter. If they are going to bring in a new man, or anything of that sort, we are all going to kick. Rogers at Lamu ought to get Mombasa & we others go up a step, but Hardinge has no mind of his own & may be induced to put some outsiders in. If he does, I shall ask Uncle George[4] to try to get me transferred to South Africa, & Sir Charles Ommaney, the Permt. Secy. to the Colonial Office, is a great friend of Mrs. Russell's, so would probably be able to do something too. It would be quite useless to stay on in this Protectorate if one is to be kept as a sort of perpetual pioneer without increase of pay or promotion.

I had a pleasant surprise the other day in the shape of the medal for "Uganda 1897-8" for "my services in the Uganda Protectorate during the Mutiny." This of course was our expedition with Sir A. Hardinge when we relieved Naivasha & the Ravine stations & sent on Harrison with 100 men which practically saved the situation in Uganda....The ribbon is pretty; I enclose a small bit. They didn't send much to go on with....

....I don't remember whether I told you some time ago of a great riot at Nairobi when the Coy. of the East African Rifles turned out en masse & attacked the Somali traders & there was a big fight. Foley, the Capt. was helpless & Ainsworth & all the others funked the job except Traill, & he had a nervous shock which stretched him out & was carried off the field for dead but has since recovered. Five Somalis were killed & some of the police, thinking it an opportunity not to be missed, waded in & murdered a Somali & took all his money &c. The ring-leaders were tried by Cator & four of them sentenced to death, others to long terms of penal servitude. I am glad to say the Govt. has at last had the pluck to enforce the sentences & the other day the four condemned men were shot before an enormous assemblage of natives & others. Hardinge had given orders that it was to be carried out with the uttermost publicity, all the natives were called in, & the native who told me said the people were "like grass in numbers." The officials didn't like the job but I think it will have an excellent effect generally. The following Monday a Nubian was shot in the same way for murder of an Mkikuyu at a camp in the Mts. beyond Fort Smith; so the law is beginning to recognize that drastic measures are a necessity in outlandish parts ....

....Our life here has been very uneventful. We had an official visit from the Judge, Cator, who stayed a few days & Gilkison came with him. When they left Hyatt, who was one of the survey party who gave me the watch, & is a brother of Whitehouse, the Chief Engineer, came up for a few days on sick leave & stayed with us, & he had barely left when Bowring, the auditor, came on an official visit so we had a round of visitors. Luckily my cashier here, Wilson, Ainsworth's brother-in-law, is a very painstaking, careful man, so that I have very little worry over my a/cs., & Bowring said the station books were the neatest & most accurate he had seen in either protectorate....

....Sir H.H. Johnstone is not making himself popular in Uganda & all who can are clearing the country like rats from a sinking ship. He is apparently oppressively obnoxious, whereas our Chief, Hardinge, looks on his job as a mere stop-gap & doesn't care what happens as long as he is not worried with details, which is rather disheartening for his Officers. The whole Administration would make an admirable foundation for one of Gilbert & Sullivan's comic operas, the Mikado wouldn't be in it. If you could only see some of the rubbish they write about, it would do for Punch. I have just received a General Circular to say that the price for a cow & a calf is Rs.75 in Uganda, & have to write an Official letter to acknowledge receipt of the Circular. It is like a lot of schoolboys playing at soldiers. A trip through Basutoland or any of the native territories in South Africa would do Hardinge & all the heads of Departments a power of good....

....P.S. I sent a copy of the "Geographical" with the account of Mackinder's[5] trip to Kenia in which you will see I am mentioned, & you will see there is now a "Hall tarn" on the map of Africa. I have the paper in pamphlet form, sent to me by Mackinder, so shall not want this journal back. I have marked approximately the situation of our new Station & the various routes to it. When the rivers are full we have a back door over the mountains to Naivasha. We are about equidistant from Kitui, Hinde's Station, Machakos & Naivasha. Nairobi is slightly further, but as Hd. Qrs. of Railway & Administration, will probably be our depot.

Machakos. Aug. 17th. 1900.

As you can see by the above address we are still in Machakos, but my men & loads should arrive here tomorrow & then we are quite ready. But apparently no one is in a hurry to get us away, for the Nubian escort has not yet been provided, nor do we know who is the Officer going in charge. A clerk also is a minor detail which they have apparently overlooked, though I requisitioned for one a month ago. We are leaving nearly everything here & only taking camp kit & actual necessaries as we intend to picnic for the next seven months & hope to get home in April. They only allow us 30 loads, & as our tents & camp gear, chairs, beds, bedding &c. amount to about 15, it does not leave much margin for 7 months provisions & clothing. In fact I reckon this move will cost us from £10 to £20 each, & as this is the second in 9 months, it comes rather heavy. The annoying part is that it is only us up-country men who have these expenses in addition to having to risk our lives amongst the natives. The coast men get houses, furniture & everything, even bedding & table ornaments free & know no danger except the climate.

Machakos. Sept 4th. 1900.

As you see we are still in Machakos. I had made all my arrangements to start, but had no word about my escort & other matters from Nairobi. So at last I decided to saddle up & go there & get things settled. As it turned out I was in luck & found Sir A. Hardinge who is off to Teheran & I was able to join a large Official dinner party to send him on his way in style from Nairobi, the Metropolis of the interior.

We had everything ready to start yesterday when an express arrived to say that I was to wait Lane's arrival to hand over the Station, & as he won't be here until 6th or 7th, I had to make my date for departure the 10th. We have a Capt. Longfield of 3rd D.Gs. going with us in Command of the Det. E.A. Rifles, a good sort, cheery companion & good sportsman, so I think we shall have a good time....

....Col. Ternan, who used to be in Uganda, is to be Deputy Commr. Mombasa & as far as we can understand will practically run E. Africa & there will be a Consul-General at Zanzibar, though not even Hardinge knows who succeeds him....I struck Hardinge in good humour after lunch one day & got permission for both of us to be allowed to shoot in the preserve, as otherwise we should have to go about 30 miles from the new Station to get any shooting. This is a grand thing, for we shall now be able to get our meat & excellent sport within an hour's ride....

....We only have about 65 miles to go from here, & taking things easy, as we shall have about 300 men, I hope to arrive there on the 7th morning as the rivers are now all low. The Station is called "Mbirri" (pronounced almost "Embirri"), Kenia District, & our mails will come via Nairobi, though in the address "Mbirri, Kenia Dist. E.A. Protte. Mombasa" will be quite sufficient....

....I had what might have been a very nasty accident at Nairobi. I was going to dine at the Officers' Mess, & riding up in the dark, my horse took a corner a little too short & ran into a strand of barbed wire which had been put up to keep people off the grass. When the animal touched it with his chest he swerved & plunged & the wire tore my right knee badly. However they had a medicine chest & we had it dressed quickly so that, beyond a couple of nasty jagged wounds, there were no bad effects, & this extra week's waiting will allow the wounds to heal nicely before going on my journey. It is a bit of a nuisance having two stiff legs at once, but I am in perfect health as there was no inflammation or anything of that sort, thank goodness.

Mbirri. Kenia. 18.9.00.

Just a line to let you know that we arrived here yesterday all well & are comfortably settled in camp until we can select a spot & peg out the new Station.

We have a magnificent big new tent, 13' x 10' for a bedroom, another facing it for a box room & store, & an awning in between for a dining room, so we have made ourselves very comfortable. It has been such an awful hustle & bother since we arrived & there has been such pandemonium in camp that I have not had a moment to sit down & write as I wanted to, & now I am fairly worn out. However I get rid of 300 of my porters tomorrow & then we shall have only Swahilis in camp & shall be a good deal quieter & then we may be able to collect our senses.

The natives here are all very friendly & glad to see us & I don't anticipate the slightest trouble. Pow-wows begin early & never end, & one has to bolt meals when one can get a chance. However they can't go on for ever at this high pressure, or if they do, I can't, so it must end. We have managed to buy about a ton of food since we arrived yesterday, to ration porters for the return journey, so have not done badly. We are having fresh fish for every meal out of our own river which is a great treat. They are very plentiful & unsophisticated & the men get them by dozens. As for eels you never saw anything like them, 3 & 4 lbs. each & not a bit muddy, as the water is all pure mountain stream....

....Bee has gone to bed, for both of us are rather full up with the continual noise & turmoil of something over 1000 people dancing & singing in the camp, but we have put up with it all day & now, after rationing 500 of my chaps to go back, I feel about done.

Mbirri. Oct. 16th 1900.

 Our first mails arrived 14th. & go back today so we have to do our scribbling as quick as possible.

 Since I last wrote we have had a busy time. I pegged out the new Fort on your birthday & set to work to build a shanty 20' x 16' which will eventually be our kitchen. It is very lofty & airy, & thank goodness waterproof....The house is built & the mud walls dry & we went into it on the 14th day which was pretty smart work. I have also built a store 24' x 15' & the Clerk's house 20' x 15' both of which were completed & occupied within 18 days. The men's quarters, a building 120' x 15' is almost ready, but I could not get it finished before the rain caught us.

 On the night of the 13th. the bottom of the heavens fairly fell out & we got 2 inches of rain before morning; we had 3 & a quarter inches in four nights. The heat had been oppressive, especially in tents, so that it was a relief to get cool. I got a good bit of ground cleared & broken & have already put in potatoes, onions, beans, tomatoes & mustard & cress.

 Local labour here is cheap; they are paid half a yd. of calico a day, worth about 2d, per man per day & feed themselves. In this way I have already had nearly all the stones for 2 sides of the Fort carried from the quarry about 800 yds. away, 50 or 60 people working daily, so all the work goes on at once. We have dug the mud for walls from the centre of the ditch, so do two jobs at once.

 I have been here, there & everywhere to superintend, so we have a pretty busy time, but it is interesting work & everything is going on so well. The natives are friendly & eager to earn cloth & beads & all our thatching grass has been brought in by the women which leaves my own men free to build a quarry. We catch plenty of fresh fish from our river, including eels, & guinea fowl, partridges &c. close by.

 The fowls we brought with us have so far done us well in the egg line & we buy our milk morning & evening from a native for 1 Rupee (1/4d) a month paid in cloth.

 The altitude I find is about 4500 ft. above sea level, as Mackinder puts it, & hitherto the temperature has been very equable, highest 85° & lowest 63° so there is no great change day or night. We have had some lovely views of Kenia & the scenery round is very fine. We have had no time for any shooting, but Bee & I lazed down the river one Sunday & enjoyed ourselves, though I only caught one fish....Both Bee & I are keeping awfully fit & looking forward to our trip home in March or April.

Mbirri. Nov. 19th. 1900.

A Merry Xmas & a Happy New Year & many of them to all at home. We have just come back from a little outing to finish up our shooting season. The Game Regulations have put up our licences from £3 to £10 for the year, & as mine expired on 16th., & we hope to go home on leave in March or April, I thought it not good enough to take out a fresh one & determined to have a good wind up & afterwards content myself with birds for the time being....

....The stone wall of the Fort is almost finished & I hope to have the flagstaff up soon when Bee will hoist the flag. We are at present inundated with visitors, two Europeans having come out from Nairobi & three down from a trading trip. They are not all guests, but we started a Visitors' Book a la Kikuyu & hope to get the autograph of a few celebrities....

....Our rainy season has set in fairly. We have already had radishes out of the garden & most things are coming on splendidly, but some of our seed was not good & spinach & onions are dead failures. As for weeds they are almost impossible to cope with. My greatest successes so far are vegetable marrows, cucumbers & melons, but beans & peas do well & potatoes, though these last are inclined to run to tops, they grow so fast.

I have had the painful necessity of arresting & sending for trial the only European trader[6] in the District for raiding; he has evidently had a real good time since I left Fort Smith....

....The natives around here are all very friendly & we have absolutely no trouble & I can get more labourers than I can employ; but with our beautiful red-tape system I am unable to get the coolies supplied, to pay them, so that just now they are working on credit, & in a few days I'm afraid I shall have to stop work. It is too annoying when everything is going on so splendidly. However our visitors are very surprised at the amount of work done in such a short time. Your suggestion of the name of N Bii for the Fort was strangely near the name Mbirri, which is the name of this part of the District.

Mbirri. Dec. 8th. 1900.

Just a hurried line to say that we are both fit & jolly. We have lost our bold Dragoon [Capt. Longfield], he has been shifted to other quarters & an Asst. D.O. sent out here, so I have to be Commandant of the troops amongst my other duties. Our new man "Skene"[7] is a very quiet insignificant chap with about 3 yrs. service, most of which he has spent on sick leave, but he is a gentlemanly chap & I think will do. Our latest news is that Jenner & over 60 police have been killed in Jubaland. I hope it is not true, but the troops have all been rushed off there & I hear they have sent for an Indian Regiment. If there is a war it will be a big job. Poor Jenner came into a lot of money on his father's death (Sir Wm. Jenner) & had decided to retire from this Service in April next, so it is doubly hard lines to go & get killed at the last....

....We hope to go for a picnic at Xmas to meet the Hindes on the Thika River to the east of here, but the men I sent down with letters are now about 5 days overdue, whether drowned or eaten by lions I know not, but I hope they will turn up sometime. We have had a tremendous lot of rain these last few weeks, some 17 inches or so. The garden is splendid & already we are eating beans, lettuces &c. which were planted less than 2 months ago....

....Our Fort is nearly completed & I am only waiting for a mason to start the big stone house. Bee is beginning to count the days before our leave. We may be able to catch the French Mail on 27th March from Zanzibar, but as my 30 months are not really up until 31st March, it is quite possible that we shall only be able to go by 27th April boat. In fact I should think this most probable. This would get us home on 15th May & we shall have 4 & a half months clear at home. I shall probably know before we go what the chances are of promotion, if any, & make plans accordingly.

Mbirri. Jany. 21st. 1901.

My Dear old Dad,

I was under the impression that I had written to you since our return from our Xmas picnic, but Bee says not, so I suppose she is right. I have been so busy that I don't know what I wrote & what I didn't.

We had a very jolly Xmas picnic with the Hindes in an entirely new part of the country. I took out a special licence to shoot game for 14 days which cost 30 Rupees, or £2 in white man's money. This is rather a lot but I had my money's worth out of it. We arranged to meet on the Thika River, the boundary of our respective Districts & met there two days before the time agreed on.

It is a splendid country for game, for no Europeans have been there before, so Hinde & I had a good time & Bee & Mrs. H. enjoyed themselves hugely & talked themselves hoarse. I had bad luck the first day I saw lions, chiefly I must confess through excessive caution. I saw six in the morning & never bagged one. However on Xmas Eve Hinde & I went out & I bagged a good lioness, too close for Hinde's idea of sport, though she was fully 100 yds. off & going all she knew. I also shot an ostrich that day, & another day shot a very big hippo. So with a few antelope I worked out my licence. We had a really good Xmas dinner & came home on 27th., arriving 3 days later.

After seeing in the New Year & Century I went off to Meranga, North of the Tana, to settle disputes between Hinde's Wakamba, who had followed me here, & the natives of the District. On my return I had to summons two Europeans who were here for breach of the Game Regulations. This meant a lot of work & investigation, & at last I sent Skene, my Asst. to Nairobi to give his evidence & watch the case, as I can only commit a case of this sort against Europeans to the higher court. My last criminal case against one Boyes for dacoity fell through for want of witnesses, though I sent 19 witnesses in. I fancy there is a game on somewhere & have therefore written direct to the Judge to have the matter enquired into & someone will hear more about it.

I have applied for leave to get away by the April French Mail, so we hope to be home about 15th May, as I think they cannot delay me.

A good old friend of ours, Tommy Watson, the head of the E.A. Scottish Mission, who formerly lived at Kibwezi & afterwards brought the Mission to Kikuyu, died of pneumonia in December. It was a terrible shock to both of us; he was such a good little chap & always a welcome guest in old Fort Smith. It is not unlikely that we shall escort Mrs. Watson[8] home. They had only been married nine months. Charters, Wilson & Watson; three heads of that Mission whom I have known go under. The old hands out here are getting rapidly less & less & I am afraid there is no chance of the insurance Coy. letting me off my premium after last year's experience.

I have been a bit seedy, chill on the liver after wading the Tana River up to my neck, but I think it is passing off now. We are both counting the days like children & looking forward to a good time at home.

With best love to all.

Ever your affectionate son.

Francis G. Hall.

Notes

1. Harry Stanley Tompkins, administrative officer in Uganda, appointed Sub-Commissioner 1904.

2. Henry Labouchere. Anti-Imperialist MP who vocally opposed the building of the Uganda Railway and the annexation of the country.

3. Charles Henry Ryall, Superintendent of Police for the Uganda Railway, was on his way to Nairobi by train to settle a strike by Indian labourers. He was accompanied by Mr. R.F.P. Huebner, a farmer, and Mr. Parenti, the Italian Vice-Consul at Mombasa. Ryall was persuaded to interrupt his journey at a place called Kima (Kiswahili for minced meat), 260 miles from the coast, to try to kill a persistently successful man-eating lion. Ryall's carriage was shunted to a siding near the station and the three men kept watch. Eventually Ryall volunteered to keep a solitary lookout while his friends slept, Parenti occupying the floor and Huebner the upper berth. It is supposed that Ryall then dozed off in the lower bunk. The man-eater jumped onto the open platform at the end of the carriage and opened the unlocked sliding door of the compartment with a paw. Due to the tilt of the carriage, the door slid shut behind him, leaving the three sleeping men in a two berth compartment with the man-eater. The lion stood on Parenti and seized Ryall in his jaws. Huebner, in the upper berth, panicked and jumped onto the lion's back to reach a second sliding door and make his escape. Unable to exit by a door, the lion crashed through a window with Ryall while Parenti jumped through the other window to seek refuge in the station. Ryall's remains were found next morning in the bush and taken to Nairobi for burial. In the old Nairobi cemetery is a memorial to Ryall. It reads, "Died June 6th 1900. Attacked whilst sleeping and killed by a man-eating lion at Kima." The lion was caught soon afterwards in a trap. He was put on show for several days and then shot.

4. George H. Goschen (later Viscount Goschen), Chancellor of the Exchequer in Lord Salisbury's Government.

5. Halford John Mackinder (later Sir Halford) was a noted geographer of the day. With two Italian guides he was the first European to climb Mt. Kenya.

6. John Boyes, 26 year old Yorkshireman who spent two years living with the Kikuyu in Karuri's village of Tuthu at the foot of the Aberdare mountains. He traded beads and cloth for flour which he sold to forts and railway survey crews. He was a fluent Kikuyu speaker and became blood brother of several influential headmen. Francis Hall and Capt. Longfield arrested Boyes on five capital charges, subsequently reduced to one, dacoity, at his trial in Nairobi. Hall sent no European witness to testify and the all white jury acquitted Boyes.

7. Ralph Rangabe Felix Henry Skene, Assistant Collector, Mbirri.

8. Mrs Watson stayed on for 24 years in Kikuyu, working for the religious and educational needs of the Kikuyu people.

Afterword

Extract from a letter of Dr. W. Radford of Nairobi to Colonel Hall.

Mbirri. March 26. 1901

Dear Sir,
Long before this reaches you, the sad news of your son's death will have been communicated to you. It is almost impossible for one to describe the loss that his colleagues have sustained. Hall was so well known here & in Uganda and had endeared himself to all. His kindness, tact and consideration at once attracted me, and his thorough manliness and honesty were a byword. I can safely say no man in this country ever had such influence with natives as he; his name was a talisman and his memory will live long among the Wakikuyu as a man to be feared, respected and loved.

He left this Station last February to punish certain tribes living some days away, but was seized with dysentery almost at once. Only his pluck and great sense of duty sustained him for a week, but at last he was compelled to return to his Station in a most critical state. Mrs. Hall & Mr. Skene nursed him for some days & then decided to send into Nairobi for medical assistance. On my arrival here I found my patient too ill to be moved, so remained with him, & during this interval Mr. Skene bridged several rivers and made other arrangements to facilitate his removal. But complications set in and he passed away quite peacefully on the evening of the 18th. inst. He was conscious almost to the end and he expressed his satisfaction at remaining in the country he knew so well and among the people he had taught and trusted.

Mrs. Hall is very weary after so many weeks of anxiety, day & night nursing, but is, I am glad to say, well. We hope to return to Nairobi within a few days where her brother Mr. Russell will meet her. She will, I imagine, settle all her affairs in E. Africa before her departure for England.

You will, I hope, excuse the brevity of this letter which is purposely short and devoid of details, but I could not omit to tell you how sincerely we all grieve with you and mourn the loss of a valued and respected brother Officer.

Letter from Bee Hall to Colonel Hall.

Mbirri. April 1st 1901.

Dear Pater,

What can I write to comfort you? I need comfort so much myself that I don't know how to mete it out to others. Dr. Radford has written to you, telling you all about our Dear's death, and I thank God, dear Pater, that my strength held out to be with him to the end. It is one of my greatest consolations to think that dear Frank died in my arms, in fact God nursed him to sleep like a little child, and that he was accepted of the Father there is no doubt, his very last words being "How bright!"

I won't dwell on all the treasured details now, as I have to try and keep my feelings under control for the sake of those around me who have been kindness itself to me. No words of mine can express the goodness and worth of Dr. Radford. He hardly ever left dear Frank day or night, and if he had been his own flesh and blood, he could not have done more for him, and Frank liked him so immensely. I have tried to thank him for his great goodness but the words all stick in my throat. I can't speak much about any of it yet, it's only a fortnight ago today that it all happened.

We have been kept up here ever since, waiting for an escort, as the natives rebelled at once. But the country has settled down a bit again so we start for Nairobi tomorrow where I meet my brother. I shall settle any business there may be to do and then go on to my great friends the Hindes at Machakos until I leave for home. They will escort me about the country so you have nothing to fear. Money I shall have enough of to settle up everything & get my ticket. Mr. & Mrs. Farrant have arrived here to take over the Station & have bought nearly everything I possess up here, which saves a great deal of porterage, & when at Machakos I shall endeavour to get rid of some more household things, not presents.

I won't write anymore now, but this is to assure you I am surrounded by good friends who are doing all they can for me, but Pater dear, my happy little home is desolate & I am so lonely. I am just longing to be home & sitting with you, telling you everything.

My best love to you & all.
Your broken hearted daughter.
Bee.

Letter from Dr. Hinde of Machakos to Colonel Hall.

Machakos. 29th April 1901.

Dear Colonel Hall,

Bee expressed a wish the other day that you should be told some particulars. She is really unfit to write, so I take it upon myself, as one of Frank's best friends in East Africa, to give you some details of the last few weeks of dear Frank's life.

My wife & I met Frank & Bee on the Tana River where our Districts touched & had a very jolly Xmas - no whites have ever been there before. Frank had some trouble with his liver but was then very fit. When I was with him he got a lioness, a pretty running shot at 250 yds. We separated on 28th Dec. & had very bad weather returning to our Stations. Frank's District as you know is new & the natives troublesome.

On the 3rd Jan. he went to visit natives & returned on the 8th suffering from a bad attack of diarrhoea which pulled him down considerably. Bee nursed him to convalescence. The natives of a place called Muruka had killed a lot of our people & Frank was very anxious to punish them before going on leave so as not to hand over his District with a punitive expedition 1st thing for a new man to do. Bee begged Frank not to go as he was not fit, but he said it was his duty & went on the 19th of February. As the natives were very treacherous, Frank had to be on guard practically every night until he got back to Mbirri on the 17th. His diarrhoea had gone on to dysentery, & in crossing a big river, he got wet & was unable to change his clothes immediately. His liver already congested, suffered accordingly. On getting home he was very ill indeed. & as there was no sign of improvement in three or four days, Bee sent to Nairobi for a Doctor who arrived having marched night & day through bad country in terrible weather.

Frank became steadily worse & weaker. On the 17th of March, the anniversary of the day he was mauled by the leopard, he congratulated them on his being alive, as he was rather superstitious about that day. He died at 10 p.m. on the evening of the 18th March quite conscious & happy. During his illness he did not recognise his danger at all & until an hour before the end he did not know he was dying. You cannot imagine how greatly Frank was loved by everyone in this country & each of us feels the loss as a personal one.

Bee has been with us for the last few weeks. Her pluck is extraordinary when one thinks what she has gone through mentally & physically & we know what a devoted couple they were. If there is anything more you would like to hear, let me know.

Extract from a letter of Mr. Stallabrass to Henry Rivers.

Nairobi. 16.6.01.

The first news I got when I came back was of Hall's death. Everyone is much upset about it. I think he was the most popular man out here, & it's so bad for his wife who is such a ripping good sort & who deserves good luck if ever anyone did.

You will be glad to hear that Mbirri where he died is to be called Fort Hall. A memorial brass is to be placed in the Church at Mombasa. A public subscription is being got up for it. A man like Hall simply cannot be replaced & it makes one so sick to see the sort they send out nowadays.

Brass Memorial in Mombasa Cathedral.

'Sacred to the Memory of FRANCIS GEORGE HALL District Officer East Africa Protectorate who died at Fort Hall in the Kenia District 18th March 1901 aged 40 years.

Also of his brother-in-law EDWARD JOHN HENDERSON RUSSELL Assistant District Officer East Africa Protectorate who died at Shimoni in the Vanga District 31st May 1900 aged 28 years. This Brass is erected as a tribute of regard and affection by their numerous friends in East Africa."
.

COPY OF OFFICIAL NOTICE.

Mombasa. 1 June 1901.

Notice is hereby given that the Government Station at Mbirri in the Kenia District will be known Officially as FORT HALL in memory of the late Mr. Hall who founded the Station and devoted his energies to developing it until his lamented death last March.

* * * *

Bee Hall married Dr Radford and they had two sons. He became Medical Officer for Nairobi in 1904 and was appointed Senior Medical Officer in Mombasa in 1911.

* * * *